LITERATURE & SCIENCE BREAKTHROUGHS

Connecting Language and Science Skills in the Elementary Classroom

JO-ANNE LAKE

Pembroke Publishers Limited

Dedication

To Benjamin, Noah, and Avery Goslin,
May you continue to light up the lives of many with your keen interest in nature.
Love, Nana

Acknowledgments

This book is in loving memory of my father and mother, who shared their great love of nature with their family. In their later years, mom and dad would sit for long periods of time looking out their kitchen window watching the many birds that were frequent visitors in their backyard. The image of mom drawing pictures of birds and talking about their behaviors throughout the seasons inspired me for a lifetime. I have been lucky enough to have had the opportunity to share my own passion for science with the many children I have taught and to have listened and learned from them.

Thank you to my husband Maurice, my children, and my grandchildren, who are always patient when I am writing yet another book about teaching science. Thanks also to my hardworking editor Cynthia Young whose skillful suggestions have made this book an excellent resource for teaching elementary science.

In writing this book, I hope to encourage other teachers to take a keen interest in science teaching and to continue to create and share their ideas with students and colleagues alike.

© **2000 Pembroke Publishers**
538 Hood Road
Markham, Ontario, Canada L3R 3K9
www.pembrokepublishers.com

Distributed in the U.S. by Stenhouse Publishers
477 Congress Street
Portland, ME 04101
www.stenhouse.com

We acknowledge the financial support of the Government of Canada through the Book Publishing Industry Development Program (BPIDP) for our publishing activities.

Canadian Cataloguing in Publication Data

Lake, Jo-Anne
    Literature and science breakthroughs

Rev. ed.
Includes bibliographical references and index.
ISBN 1-55138-126-5

1. Science – Study and teaching (Elementary). 2. Literature and Science. I. Title. II. Title: Literature and science breakthroughs.

LB1585.L35 2000   372.3′5   C00-931558-6

Editor: Cynthia Young
Cover Design: John Zehethofer
Cover Photography: Ajay Photographics
Typesetting: JayTee Graphics

Printed and bound in Canada
9 8 7 6 5 4 3 2 1

Table of Contents

Preface

"There is no right way to teach science. It's a way of approaching the world and asking questions and learning about it. Gather monarch butterflies on milkweed plants and bring them into the school and watch them pupate and emerge from the pupa."

Suzuki

In learning science, students need time for exploring and investigating, making observations, testing ideas, time for building things, doing things over, collecting things, and more. *The Nature of Science* speaks to this learning process:

> *When students observe differences in the way things behave or get different results in repeated investigations they should suspect that something differs from trial to trial and try to find out what. Sometimes the difference results from methods, sometimes from the way the world is. The emphasis on scientific engagement calls for frequent hands-on activities. But that is not say that students must or even can discover by direct experience. Stories about people making discoveries and inventions can be used to illustrate the kinds of convictions about the world and what can be learned from it that are shared by the varied people who do science.*

I developed an interest in science teaching and learning by observing how children use their natural curiosity to learn about the world they live in. Curiosity is the spirit of scientific investigation. I have committed a lifetime to searching for new teaching strategies that nurture children's curiosity while developing the knowledge and skill described by the learning expectations for science. I have been especially interested in strategies that incorporate children's literature with hands-on experiences. My first book, *Imagine: A Literature-based Approach to Science*, outlined how to develop a program using children literature to spark an interest in science. *Literature and Science Breakthroughs: Connecting Language and Science Skills in the Elementary Classroom* extends that approach.

A variety of children's literature exists for this literature-based approach to science in the elementary classroom. With planning and thoughtful selection, a teacher can use science-focused fiction, non-fiction, and other literary styles to connect language and literature to science skills and concepts in the real world. *Literature and Science Breakthroughs* goes beyond "reading" about science, offering diverse hands-on activities that bring all aspects of science to life and help students gain first-hand experience with scientific principles. *Literature and Science Breakthroughs* is organized around five main strands in science:

Life Systems, Matter and Materials, Energy and Control, Structures and Mechanisms, and Earth and Space Systems. Throughout this book, you will find reviews and recommendations for children's literature that can be used in each of these five learning strands.

Of my twenty-five years of teaching experience (from Kindergarten to Grade 8, including the gifted program), I devoted significant efforts in the last ten years to tracking down and exploring children's books about science and technology. On my journey into the world of science books, I found there were many types of books available: storybooks, discovery and exploration books, poetry books, pop-ups, novels, big books, inquiry books, and information books. When you teach a topic in any of the strands, choosing the right types of books to support the learning is important. Sometimes, you may find that only one kind of book is suitable, while at other times the topic may be explored through many types of books.

There are many ways to use books about science and technology with children to ensure that children are afforded as many opportunities as possible to do science and technology inside and outside the classroom. *Literature and Science Breakthroughs* suggests a variety of approaches and provides a number of applications. The interconnections between knowledge, skills, and concepts strengthen children's understanding of the world. Integrating language, literature, and science provides a special key to understanding science.

Each chart shows an excerpt from one type of book for a topic in a specific strand. The literature–science and technology learning links are also indicated.

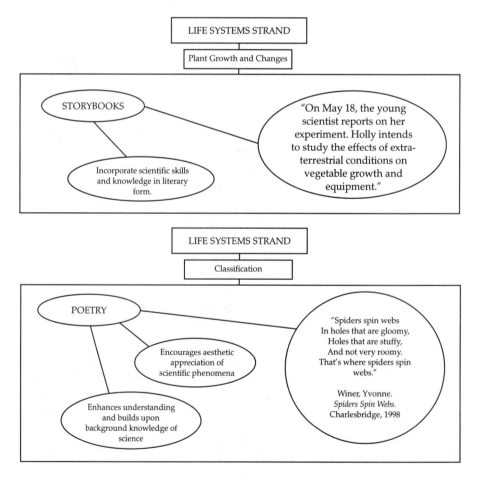

The first four chapters of *Literature and Science Breakthroughs* provide the framework for implementing a literature-based approach in teaching science. Chapter One: Sensing Wonder — Children, Teachers, and Science focuses on how both children and teachers can become caught up in the wonders of science. Chapter Two: The Literature-Based Approach for Teaching Science outlines the advantages of using the approach, providing a method for integrating literature and science. In addition, suggestions for getting started are included. Chapter Three: Linking the Literature and Hands-on Instruments discusses the kinds of instruments and opportunities to use them that a literature-based program can offer. Chapter Three also gives some concrete examples and demonstrates the methodology that teachers can use on their own. Chapter Four: Linking Science, Assessment Techniques, and Evaluation includes information about strategies, tools, and applications that are appropriate for this kind of approach. Chapter Five: The Five Strands explores the strands one by one, providing specific suggestions for the literature and hands-on activities for children to do. Chapter Six: Five Strands at Once — Cross Connections considers literature suggestions from all five strands that can be used as a model for planning an interdisciplinary approach to linking science and children's literature.

1

Sensing Wonder — Children, Teachers, and Science

"Nothing is too wonderful to be true. To have a scientific attitude toward the world one must be able to imagine wonderful things — even things that seem too wonderful to be true."

Michael Faraday
Physicist

Wonderment can captivate and challenge our senses. Wonderment stimulates questions that unlock the door to understanding science and the world around us.

In *All I Really Need to Know I Learned in Kindergarten*, Robert Fulghum, reflecting on his kindergarten experience, reminds us that allowing children to ask questions satisfies their curiosity. As well, he suggests that such questioning is the very fabric of life-long learning.

...There's a whole lot of things I don't understand about entirely — some large, some small. I keep a list, and the list gets longer and longer as I get older and older. For example, here's a few mysteries I added this year. Why do people believe that pushing an elevator button several times will make it come quicker? Why does every tree seem to have one old stubborn leaf that just won't go away?

Robert Fulghum, 1988

In the daily grind, we sometimes forget that children are, by nature, inquisitive. When children have the opportunity to use their ideas, they approach each experience with infinite curiosity: investigating, observing, questioning, discovering, exploring, figuring out, and making mistakes freely in a problem-solving environment.

An important part of students' exploration is telling others what they wonder about the things they see and think. Relying on their imagination, prior experiences, and new information and events, children construct meaning. Children form their own ideas about natural phenomena before engaging in science experiences in the classroom. When children have lots of time to talk about what they observe and to compare their observations with those of others, they can articulate their conceptual understandings in their own words.

Children's ideas are often very different from those in the scientific community.

This developmental process was modeled in one Grade Two class, which was studying bubbles for the first time. Their classroom teacher wrote in her reflective journal: "My kids actually thought the rainbow colors in bubbles were caused because we had tissue butterflies hanging on our windows. I let them experiment in different parts of the school to see if the colors were still present. The could hardly believe that they were. As a group, they finally concluded that there must be oil in bubbles, because oil has the same colors."

In planning for science experiences in the classroom, we need to tap into the children's imaginations, thereby allowing them to use their prior knowledge and experiences as they construct new meaning. We need to value the nature and detail of children's concepts of the world and to understand how they develop their sometimes "inventive" meanings for scientific ideas and words.

As teachers in today's world, we need to understand that ways of thinking and doing are just as important in science as acquiring bodies of knowledge. Our role is to make learning more meaningful. To achieve this, we need to actively seek out, observe, listen, learn, and identify the ways in which students understand particular scientific ideas. We can then use this information to modify and extend the children's learning and understanding. We must also *inspire* children's interest in science while helping them to link new facts, concepts, and process/inquiry skills that will help them discover what they want to know. Teachers in science classrooms must emphasize thinking and problem-solving skills. We must ensure that children develop scientific "habits of mind" — curiosity, questioning, open-mindedness, persistence, and learning from errors — for these will promote exploration and discovery.

The same message came from Herbert Spencer in 1850, when he said, "Children should be led to do their own investigations. They should be told as little as possible and induced to discover as much as possible." Sadly, this is not what is happening in science in the majority of elementary classrooms. The gap between theory and practice in science education remains firmly planted. Susan Black's research ("Science Lessons," *The American School Board Journal,* 1999) states, "By the time students graduate, they might be able to identify five types of deciduous trees and sketch the human skeletal system, but they seldom get around to learning important science concepts such as diversity among species and adaptation." While it is necessary to acquire factual knowledge, it is more important that children understand the conceptual framework that relates these facts to each other and to the world in which the children live. (*Science Through Children's Literature — An Integrated Approach,* Carol Butzow and John Butzow. Teacher Ideas Press, 1989.) Immersion in the concept is necessary for students to generate questions and answers, read from a great variety of science-related books, generate more questions, and still have time for hands-on exploration and discovery.

The National Science Education Standards (National Research Council, 1996) indicates that students should spend less time memorizing facts and more time reasoning and solving problems. The standards stipulate that children should learn in cooperative groups, use more hands-on materials, and study only a few science concepts in more depth. As teachers, we are constantly struggling in science to strike a balance between building a knowledge base and conducting investigations. Building a knowledge base gives students more information and reduces the amount of time we commit to science. Conducting investigations allows students to find the information themselves. It requires a greater time commitment from both the teacher and the students, for children need time to research and explore in an inquiry approach. Astonishingly, both these methods of instruction share a common goal in science teaching and learning — teaching important concepts in-depth in order for students to reach an understanding. It seems time is the biggest barrier to achieving the ideal classroom learning environment in science.

My hope is that teachers will be released from time barriers and make a commitment to helping children become scientifically literate. Effective education for developing scientific literacy requires every student to be frequently and actively involved in exploring nature and the world in ways that incorporate how scientists work.

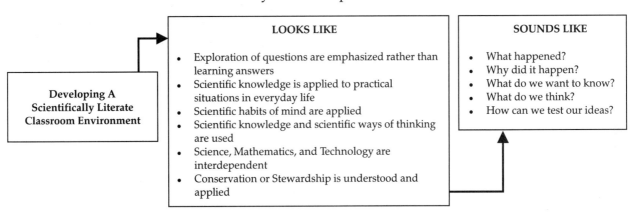

There is no better time to communicate the scientific attitude than during childhood, and no better way than with good quality children's books. For example, in *A City in Winter* Mark Helprin's rich narrative is supported by Chris van Allsburg's lush illustrations. Children will be enchanted as you read this compelling story that actively incorporates a number of topics in the strands.

A City in Winter could be used to introduce *or* reinforce scientific information, habits of mind, concepts, and skills.

> I was in a vast room at the base of thirty stories of gleaming machinery that turned the hands of the four clock faces.
>
> That which was not brass was gold; that not nickel, silver; that not glass, diamond or sapphire. The motive power for this machine...was most extraordinary. A circular chain of platinum rods was draped over a geared wheel, all of gold, the size of a barn. Where the links of the chain were joined, a huge jewel the size of a melon was held in a mount. When the light of an electric arc pulsed through a battery of gems above and struck the jewels on the chain, the chain moved...
>
> As it moved, it generated the electricity that turned it, with much power left over. This...was a perpetual motion machine, which, it was widely believed, could not exist.

This passage alone relates to several topics: rocks and minerals (brass, gold, silver, nickel, diamond, sapphire); structures (a vast room of thirty stories); pulleys and gears (circular chain...was draped over a geared wheel); electricity (the light of an electric arc...generated the electricity that turned it); and motion and movement (machinery that turned the hands of the four clock faces...This was a perpetual motion machine...). Fiction, non-fiction, or activity books — all are appropriate when they help students achieve the expectations. What a wonderful way to ignite and maintain the children's curiosity and interest!

Research endorses the use of literature for teaching literacy. Using children's literature with a science focus allows children to bring their own background experiences to the text and extend their understanding of concepts and skills in an environment that facilitates a constructivist viewpoint, values inquiry, and encourages active learning. This understanding transfers and extends naturally in the home.

2

The Literature-Based Approach to Teaching Science

There is no better time to acquire scientific habits of mind and no better instigator than quality children's books. Children's books that instill the habits of mind sustain science.

Using children's literature with a science focus allows children to bring their own background of experiences to the text and extend their understanding of concepts and skills in the classroom. This understanding transfers and extends naturally in the home. When literature is used to teach science, the benefits are two-fold. Literacy is encouraged and science is at the front-line. This language-based approach to science instruction helps teachers apply their language arts skills, linking them to children's science learning.

Advantages of Using Literature in a Science Program

When Albert was ten years old, his uncle gave him a book on geometry. Albert read the book through, and then he read it again and again. Soon he saw order in the whole universe. This book made him feel so excited that he could scarcely wait for the geometry class that had just opened in his school. The first day in that class, Albert revealed an understanding of geometry that went far beyond the book.

There are many advantages to choosing science-focused literature, rather than a textbook, in teaching elementary science. These advantages, listed here, are further elucidated through suggested applications of real children's literature.

- *Science-focused literature introduces science concepts through the language and illustrations within the context of story.*
The Night Book by Pamela Hickman and *How Do Animals Adapt?* by Bobbie Kalman use rich text, hands-on exploratory activities, and colorful illustrations to introduce the concept of adaptation. In Hickman's book, children find out why some animals come out only after dark. Questions such as, "Why do animals adapt?" and ideas for children to explore such as "Adapting to the dark" provide many opportunities for children to investigate the concept.

- *Science-focused literature helps children to develop their imagination through exploring and investigating science principles.*
Einstein was once asked how to help a child who was gifted in math. He answered, "Read him the great myths of the past. Stretch his

13

imagination." One of the goals of establishing an effective elementary science program is building an environment open to inquiry and supportive of imagination.

How Do Flies Walk Upside Down? by Melvin and Gilda Berger invites children to explore, among other things, the characteristics, senses, eating habits, and life cycle of different insects, and provides children with lots of opportunity to use their imagination. Beginning with a question in title, the authors immediately and actively engage children in solving a problem. Through observation and hands-on investigation of flies and other creatures, there is opportunity for children to question and ascertain the reality of science, while using their sense of the fantastic.

• *Science-focused literature encourages integration with other subject areas.*
Many children's books, while focusing on one topic, offer insight and knowledge of topics beyond the main focus. A variety of activity-based experiences that emerge from children's literature integrate science across the curriculum more effectively. *Kites—Magic Wishes That Fly Up to the Sky* by T. Demi primarily explores kite making, but also links the Energy and Control strand with other areas of the curriculum. History is explicit in the story's setting in ancient China where kite making was a tradition.

• *Science-focused literature provides up-to-date scientific information.*
Textbooks are printed for new curriculum, which does not always coincide with new developments in scientific knowledge. A textbook is often intended for use over a number of years, and scientific developments may not be included until the next curriculum call results in a new textbook. Using children's literature for science can help teachers find the most up-to-date books at a variety of reading and interest levels for a variety of science topics. The diversity and number of children's books can give educators ongoing access to current information.

For example, *The Incredible Journey To The Centre Of The Atom: The Incredible Journey To The Edge Of The Universe* provide two stories in one. It allows you to follow the journey from universe to particle and, when you reach the end, turn the book over and follow the journey from particle to universe. This book works well in the Earth and Space strand, particularly when children are studying the Solar System.

• *Science-focused literature provides teachers with an opportunity to build knowledge quickly.*
Teachers can quickly read fiction and nonfiction books on any science topic, in order to learn new information, reinforce existing knowledge, or extend their learning in preparation for planning science opportunities in the classroom.

Joanna Cole's *The Magic School Bus Inside the Earth* provides teachers with a quick look at rocks and minerals. Associated vocabulary is introduced throughout the text, and facts on the topic are recorded and can be previewed at a glance. A complete picture of a student rock collection and a vocabulary chart at the end of the book provide reference for teachers and students to reflect on their learning.

- *Science-focused literature helps children make connections and see relationships among the topics they are studying.*

Special techniques in children's literature, such as providing working models and tools for hands-on activities as an integral part of the text encourage children to connect specific skills and instruments with ways of learning and finding out more, and also help them see how different science topics and science disciplines are related.

Wetlands Nature Search — A hands-on guide for nature sleuths includes a real magnifying glass. Supplying a special hands-on instrument helps children get closer to nature, while at the same time honing their observation skills. Using the hand lens children can locate tiny creatures and master mazes to locate the animal that doesn't belong.

- *Science-focused literature connects related issues, topics, and sub-topics in science.*

The introduction of a broad topic in science through children's literature may lead to the discovery of one small, specific sub-topic for children to explore in detail. Familiarity with a wide variety of literature on a broad topic will assist both teachers and children in organizing their thoughts for selecting a sub-topic to investigate.

Our Big Home by Linda Glaser introduces the broad topic "Earth is a large home." This book is very useful in the Structures and Mechanisms strand. Organizing materials for a focus on structures can be relatively easy if you are familiar with additional related children's literature. *Up Goes The Skyscraper!* by Gail Gibbons, *This Is My House* by Arthur Dorros, and *Animal Homes* by Barbara Taylor are just a few of the available titles for getting started on learning more about structures.

- *Science-focused literature encourages activity-based science experiments.*

Activity-based opportunities naturally emerge from science-focused children's literature. Hands-on opportunities initiated by the text encourage children to explore and discover science concepts through manipulating materials. *Science With Water* by Helen Edom invites the development of science experiences at a water table. In playing with a variety of materials in water, children naturally explore sinking, floating, absorbing, and dissolving.

- *Science-focused literature provides multi-sensory experiences.*

Multi-sensory experiences can be introduced through specific children's books. Auditory, visual, and tactile opportunities built naturally into the text draw into the learning by using their senses.

Children's literature has the capacity to focus on more than one of our five senses. Peter Riley's *Our Mysterious Ocean as it's never been seen before!* taps into a child's tactile sensory mode. Children can take a see-through tour in a watery world — going from coral reefs to ocean trenches. Many children and adults learn when what they read taps into their multi-sensory capabilities.

- *Science-focused literature provides motivation to learn.*

There are many special effect books that motivate children to learn through the element of surprise.

Shar Levine's *3-D Bees and Micro Fleas* allows children to see insects magnified up to 400,000 times through the use of a 3-D viewer. Children can see fascinating species close-up in spectacular 3-D through the attachment.

- *The variety of book types and literary styles found in science-focused literature encourages the understanding of science.*

Children's literature encompasses a number of book types, as well as literary styles, including big books, novels, storybooks, poetry books, pop-up books, inquiry books, information books, discovery and exploration books, and books on the environment.

Some children learn better when new material is introduced through poetry/verse. The rhythm catches their attention, cementing their understanding of the science concepts. *Have You Seen Bugs?* by Joanne Oppenheim uses a verse format to help students learn. The rhyming text and illustrations support our understanding of a bug's life. Other children, however, learn by doing. Pop-up books present opportunities for hands-on investigation of working models that provide meaningful experiences for these children. Still other children find the singing and chanting inherent in some books are helpful to the learning process. Using a variety of books that spans the interest of every child offers many opportunities for children to succeed in building a better conceptual understanding of science.

- *Science-focused children's literature conveys meaning through illustrations.*

Meaning is implicit in the vivid and detailed illustrations unique to children's literature. *I Spy Treasure Hunt* is a book of picture riddles inviting children to play a familiar game — I Spy. Clues presented in very brief text is supported by the illustrations of objects the reader is asked to find.

- *Science-focused children's literature introduces hands-on instruments through text and illustrations.*

Hands-on instruments are introduced naturally through children's literature. *The Best Book of Fossils, Rocks and Minerals* by Chris Pellant introduces materials and science instruments, such as a rock hammer, through illustrations and the accompanying text. The introduction of hands-on instruments encourages children to explore their use and function, which may lead to further examination of other items that are used for performing scientific tasks.

- *Science-focused literature serves as a catalyst to link skills.*

Process skills developed through science can be integrated into all parts of our lives. Since strategies in learning to read and learning science are similar, children's literature can link these skills.

  - Observing: using the senses to gather information about objects and events
  - Classifying: organizing information into logical categories
  - Seriating: arranging items or events according to a characteristic
  - Communicating: receiving and expressing information through listening, speaking, writing, reading, viewing, and presenting

- Measuring: comparatively or quantitatively describing the length, area, volume, mass, or temperature of objects
- Inferring: reaching conclusions based on evidence and reasoning, without direct observation
- Predicting: estimating the outcome of an event based on observation
- Hypothesizing: providing a possible explanation based on a number of observations and inferences
- Experimenting: designing and performing exploratory investigations to probe predictions or hypotheses
- Controlling variables: discovering and manipulating the situations and/or environments that determine the results of an experiment
- Interpreting: drawing conclusions about the data gathered
- Making models: constructing actual or creative representations of items using a variety of materials
- Manipulating equipment and materials: using appropriate commercial or homemade tools and supplies for investigative purposes

In, *First Field Guide Rocks and Minerals* rocks and crystals are classified into groups. Children learn the classification scheme through working hands-on with specimens and magnifiers.

- *The broad range of children's literature ensures higher success in understanding science skills and concepts through reaching all developmental stages.*

Children are at different developmental stages when they arrive at school. In developing concepts, each child has a different starting point that is determined by previous experiences and understanding. Having children draw a profile of themselves is one indicator in helping us understand these differences.

The three children whose work is featured here are at different stages of development, even though they are the same chronological age and have been in the same classroom since the beginning of the year. Clearly, these profiles indicate the varying needs of the children we teach. Whether in the very early stages of growth and development (Figure A) or in the more advanced stage of growth and development (Figures B and C), children's literature can enhance each child's understanding of science concepts at his or her level of development.

In developing the concept of sinking and floating, Henry Pluckrose's *Think about Floating and Sinking* provides experiences with hands-on materials for children in the early stages of development. Neil Ardley extends these basic concepts in *The Science Book of Water* by providing problem-solving and decision-making situations that allow children to explore, discover, and build a stronger conceptual base. At a more advanced level, Joanna Cole's *The Magic School Bus at the Waterworks*, a book rich in language and illustrations, leads to numerous activities that explore the nature of water.

In meeting the needs of all children, traditional science textbooks cannot offer the same range as children's literature. With current emphasis on meeting the needs of all children, it is a priority to provide a wide variety of fiction and nonfiction materials from which children can select.

Children engage in and learn best when activities and literature are matched to their stage of development. Teachers using children's literature as an approach to teaching science are comfortable in knowing that they can teach science effectively without a rigorous scientific background. In making the transition from science textbook to children's literature, the selection of the best science books is critical.

Figure A

Figure B

Figure C

Selecting and Organizing the Literature

The Role of the Teacher

- Refer to the information in this chapter of the book.
- Take along a copy of the criteria for selecting the best science books when you begin your search.
- Read the books yourself before choosing to use them in the classroom.
- Select books that will strengthen children's understanding of science concepts and skills.
- Think about real-world connections that the book might offer for further class discussion.
- Become familiar with the "habits of mind" that scientists demonstrate and search for books that will provide opportunities for children to role model them as they do science.

"Useful books provide information, but stories have the magic in them that make you run out into the backyard at night and stare up into infinity to see what's there." (Twain, *The Adventures of Huckleberry Finn*, 1884) Familiarity with Twain's message helps us make selections of fiction and nonfiction books that are entertaining, inviting, and exciting — books that grab children's attention. If they are chosen carefully, the excitement of discovery these books can generate is irreplaceable. Children gravitate naturally to exciting books.

The first step in your search is to become familiar with a wide variety of children's literature, including fiction and nonfiction. As you read, remember the wisdom of C. S. Lewis when he says, "No book is really worth reading at the age of 10 which is not really worth reading at the age of 50."

Fiction gives a perspective that allows children to know facts in another way, and to confirm what they are learning from informational sources (*Huck, 1987*). Effective literature-based science programs include a variety of resources from both fiction and nonfiction. When making your selections, employ a list of criteria to ensure your selection consists of the best science-focused books for your classroom. Use of these criteria helps to avoid a "watered-down" science program.

Butterfly House by Eve Bunting is a perfect example of the function and use of fiction in a literature-based science program. The strong storyline enables children to understand the life of a butterfly. Relevant vocabulary and specific facts about the butterfly are introduced in the context of the story. Text and illustrations reveal the butterfly's appearance, habitat, and other pertinent information. Children are encouraged to extend their senses by using magnifiers to observe and describe the butterfly, reinforcing hands-on investigation.

Nonfiction books provide accurate information that is consistent with current scientific knowledge and that reinforces the skills and concepts uncovered in fiction. *Eyewitness Books Insects* by Laurence Mound provides an alternative to an encyclopedia. Real-life photographs and captions provide a fresh look at insects. Labeled diagrams, colored illustrations, and specific inquiry questions found embedded in the text work together to provide a clear description of the butterfly and many other insects.

As you read children's literature, ask yourself the following questions. Your response will help you choose the best books for encouraging science teaching.

1. Is there a strong science thread running through the text and illustrations?

There are many children's books that lend themselves to science teaching and learning. Our task is to find them and to determine the degree of science content in each book. Read each book carefully. Can the science content be determined easily in the text and illustrations? *Archaeologists Dig For Clues* by Kate Duke is an excellent example of fiction with a strong science thread woven throughout the story. The whole process of an archaeological dig is outlined clearly within the storyline. Classroom experiences, using hands-on materials and equipment, help to replicate the real-life process. Related activity cards, stemming from the children's interests and developed in partnership with the teacher, emphasize student learning.

2. *Are there opportunities in the text and illustrations to enhance science skills?*

The skills developed through science teaching help children make sense of their experiences. Children learn to observe, classify, seriate, communicate, measure, infer, predict, hypothesize, experiment, control variables, interpret, manipulate materials, and make models. Appropriate science literature emphasizes these skills within the text and illustrations.

The books in the following chart focus on the skill of classification. (The list is by no means exhaustive.)

Children's Literature — Developing the Skill of Classification	
Author	**Title**
Joanna Cole	*The Magic School Bus Lost in the Solar System*
Jonathan D.W. Kahl	*First Field Guide Weather*
Yvonne Winer	*Spiders Spin Webs*
Louise Osborne & Carol Gold	*Solids, Liquids And Gases*
Claire Llewellyn	*Mighty Machines — Truck*

In *The Magic School Bus Lost in the Solar System* Cole presents classification as a useful skill. She teaches the development of this skill within the text by presenting individual pages from student notebooks that focus on one planet. The book culminates with a summary chart classifying all the planets according to size, distance, and other characteristics. The text, "In the classroom, we made a terrific chart of the planets and a mobile of the solar system," works in harmony with the student creation of the solar system mobile to demonstrate the use of classification as a real world skill.

First Field Guide by Jonathan Kahl speaks to everything children might want to know about weather. Numerous opportunities are provided for children to practice the skill of classification (for example, sorting and classifying clouds: cirrus, cirrocumulus, cirrostratus, altocumulus, altostratus, stratus, cumulus).

Spiders Spin Webs by Yvonne Winer presents a stunning variety of spiders and their webs. Through reading this story, children are compelled to go spider and/or web hunting. They take glee in classifying and investigating spiders and webs for their differences. In classifying webs, children may want to take a piece of black paper and guide the web towards the paper until it sticks or spray the webs and make a spider web classification book.

Solids, Liquids and Gases by Louise Osborne and Carol Gold provides many opportunities for children to identify and classify objects as solids, liquids, or gases according to the characteristics of the object.

Mighty Machines — Truck by Claire Llewellyn provides a close-up look at working machines. Children can classify each machine by name or by the number of simple machines it incorporates, or children might simply create their own classification system — based on the special characteristics of the machines.

Introducing children to a selection of books primarily for the development of the skill of classification is only a preliminary measure. To further strengthen children's understanding and their use of classification, children need to have opportunities to see, discuss, and use some different classification systems. They need time and opportunity to develop their own individual systems of classification. As their understanding increases, they will move on to more complex systems of classification.

3. *Does the text incorporate vocabulary familiar to science teaching?*

Complex scientific vocabulary can be clearly understood through the use of text and excellent detailed illustrations.

Vocabulary specific to science is introduced through books such as *Optical Tricks* by Walter Wicks, which provides meaning in context. Wicks introduces reflections, illusions, and camouflage to challenge children to compare true perceptions with false perceptions in the world of light and color. Children are encouraged to think, observe, and reflect upon specific features within their knowledge and understanding of light and color concepts.

4. *Do the illustrations and text introduce hands-on material reflecting and encouraging their use in an activity-based environment?*

Reading the literature carefully leads to a better understanding of the hands-on equipment that children need in order to explore the world. Effective science programs use the literature in connection with hands-on experiences. Science-focused literature introduces and encourages the use of such instruments.

Hands-on science activities consolidate and extend skills after they have been explored in children's stories. Linking the hands-on equipment with the text is a simple way to determine what equipment you need in order to emphasize this component of a science program.

Wetlands Nature Search by Andrew Langley introduces the use of a hand lens as a magnifier. Learning opportunities may include making magnification instruments from found materials and using hand lenses appropriately.

5. *Have I chosen books that provide a balance in opportunities for all of the science strands?*

Selecting a wide variety of children's literature for science teaching can be a positive experience for the classroom teacher. Place a strong emphasis on organizing the literature for classroom use. It should encourage easy access by both the students and the teacher. Good organization is critical to the success of the science program.

One way to begin organizing, is to establish a way to categorize the number of books that are relevant to one specific science strand. Sticky letters (E and S — Earth and Space, etc.) can be placed on the outside cover of the book. As you collect and categorize your books, work towards striking a balance between the five strands.

6. *Do my selections reflect a variety of literary genres?*

There are many kinds of science-focused books. As you read these books randomly, make a conscious effort to include a variety of genres. Look for books that encourage science learning through rhyme, story, illustration, special effects, inquiry, reference, technology, connections, models, and creativity books. You may want to add additional categories.

7. *What scientific principle and/or concept is projected?*

Good children's literature leads to an understanding of basic principles. Vicki Cobb's *Why Can't You Unscramble an Egg?* employs a series of questions and experiments. Through reading this book and through related hands-on experiences, children will come to understand concepts about the nature of matter.

8. *Have I considered including a variety of special effects books in my selections?*

Unusual artistic techniques in the text or illustrations of children's literature provide added interest and assist children in understanding science concepts. There are several special effects books available with a variety of special effects techniques.

The Incredible Journey to the Edge of the Universe and The Incredible Journey to the Centre of the Atom by Nicholas Harris and Joanna Turner. There are two books here between these covers. The book allows you to follow the journey from universe to particle through the eyes of the observer. Then, when you reach the end, turn the book over and follow the journey from particle to universe. On the second journey, your guide is a scientist, who describes and explains what you see from page to page.

Bugs and Slugs by Judy Tatchell uses lift the flaps for children to look behind leaves and under stones, open out the patterned wing of a butterfly, or follow the shiny trail of a snail. Children will be delighted as they discover of the world around them.

Nick Bantock's *A Pop-Up Book of Things That Fly* presents spectacular three-dimensional pop-ups and pull-tabs that show children how wings really work on everything from bats and dragonflies to fighter planes and supersonic jets.

Using the Literature in the Classroom

Discovering new ways for bringing science to the classroom by using the literature is half the fun. I like to view the starting points in science as "angles of sight" that have the potential to captivate and immerse children in doing science and using technology. I have a variety of angles of sight, for example, *Author, Book Type, Skill, Learning Expectation, Concept,* any of which are useful starting points for launching a science experience in your classroom.

Angles of Sight

Author Perspective

You may want to use a particular science author to lead children to science and technology, for example, Joanna Cole. Cole's *The Magic School Bus Inside the Earth* supports an environment conducive to learning science and technology. This storybook profiles a place where there is easy access to hands-on materials and a focus on inquiry as an important part of planning and executing meaningful opportunities for children. The literature encourages them to investigate rocks, minerals, and fossils in a hands-on learning environment. Classroom applications of this book are endless. In addition to starting their own rock collections, children may want to make models of caves or search for and preserve fossils as representations of their learning.

Using Cole's science series provides children with numerous opportunities to get inside the Earth, the solar system, the ocean floor, the time of the dinosaurs, a hurricane, a beehive, electricity, and more. The key is to use the literature as a link to the hands-on instruments introduced in the text and illustrations. Cole's books provide a recipe for science and technology success. Using her works, children are assured active participation in discovery, explorative, and investigative hands- on learning experiences in the classroom.

Teachers should become familiar with the works of the best science authors many of them whom I have identified through their works within this book.

Book Type Perspective

Using any one of the book types (storybooks, inquiry books, information books, discovery, and exploration books) for your angle of sight can provide multiple opportunities for engaging children in science. A system for identifying the different types of books in your classroom library (such as IN for Inquiry Books) can be helpful to both you and the children. It is important to use a wide variety of book types to meet the needs of all children. *Literature and Science Breakthroughs* looks at a diverse selection of children's books and provides 300 titles of the best science and technology related books. (Chapter Five provides a composite list of these books in the Literature Based Webs for each of the five strands.)

The Role of the Teacher

- Make science author collections available to the children.
- Make sure hands-on instruments are easily accessible to the children.
- Develop hands-on activities linking the literature with the hands-on instruments.
- Role model your active involvement in the life of the classroom.

In the examples following, an excerpt taken directly from a book illustrates the type of book and the literature/science and technology links in the specific example.

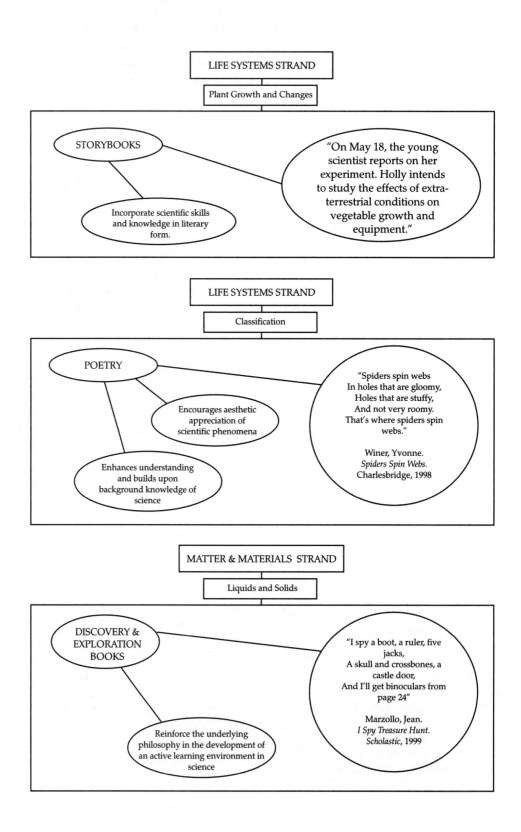

LIFE SYSTEMS STRAND

Plant Growth and Changes

STORYBOOKS

Incorporate scientific skills and knowledge in literary form.

"On May 18, the young scientist reports on her experiment. Holly intends to study the effects of extra-terrestrial conditions on vegetable growth and equipment."

LIFE SYSTEMS STRAND

Classification

POETRY

Encourages aesthetic appreciation of scientific phenomena

Enhances understanding and builds upon background knowledge of science

"Spiders spin webs
In holes that are gloomy,
Holes that are stuffy,
And not very roomy.
That's where spiders spin webs."

Winer, Yvonne.
Spiders Spin Webs.
Charlesbridge, 1998

MATTER & MATERIALS STRAND

Liquids and Solids

DISCOVERY & EXPLORATION BOOKS

Reinforce the underlying philosophy in the development of an active learning environment in science

"I spy a boot, a ruler, five jacks,
A skull and crossbones, a castle door,
And I'll get binoculars from page 24"

Marzollo, Jean.
I Spy Treasure Hunt.
Scholastic, 1999

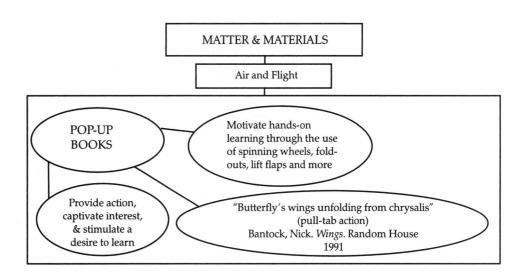

MATTER & MATERIALS

Air and Flight

POP-UP BOOKS

Motivate hands-on learning through the use of spinning wheels, fold-outs, lift flaps and more

Provide action, captivate interest, & stimulate a desire to learn

"Butterfly's wings unfolding from chrysalis" (pull-tab action)
Bantock, Nick. *Wings.* Random House 1991

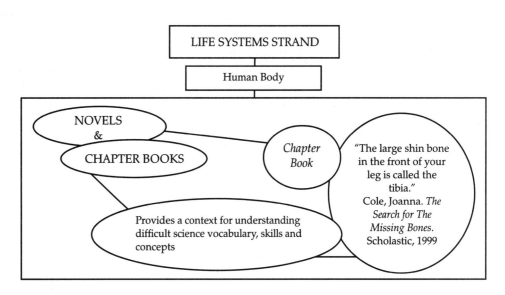

LIFE SYSTEMS STRAND

Human Body

NOVELS & CHAPTER BOOKS

Chapter Book

"The large shin bone in the front of your leg is called the tibia."
Cole, Joanna. *The Search for The Missing Bones.* Scholastic, 1999

Provides a context for understanding difficult science vocabulary, skills and concepts

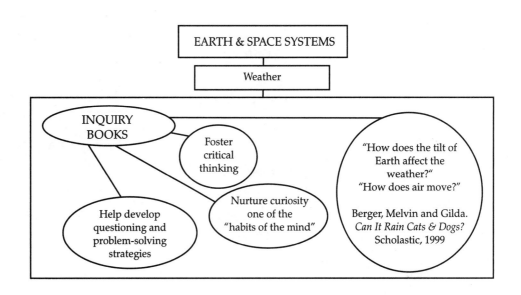

EARTH & SPACE SYSTEMS

Weather

INQUIRY BOOKS

Foster critical thinking

Nurture curiosity one of the "habits of the mind"

Help develop questioning and problem-solving strategies

"How does the tilt of Earth affect the weather?"
"How does air move?"

Berger, Melvin and Gilda. *Can It Rain Cats & Dogs?* Scholastic, 1999

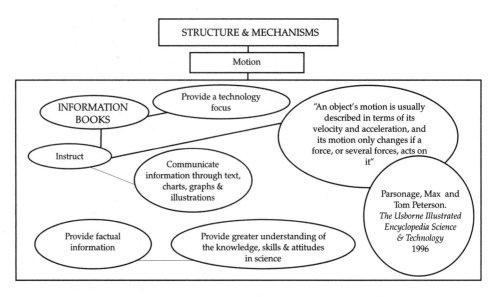

The Elders Are Watching by Dave Bouchard is an excellent poetry resource that encourages preservation of the environment. Bouchard's approach to our present predicament helps children acquire an appreciation for and understanding of a past generation. His style awakens an interest in how we can contribute to a healthier environment today. Concepts covered in the book include:

• We need to preserve our natural resources.
• Natural resources are not limitless.
• Each individual can help to preserve our world.

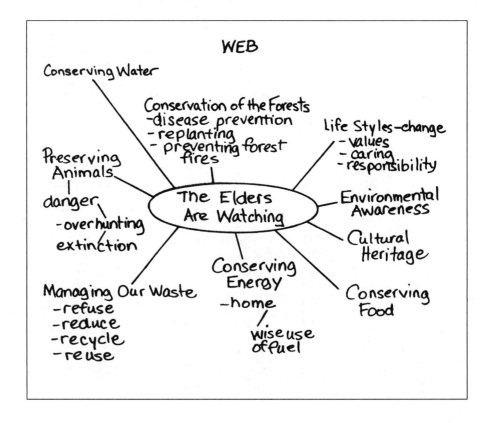

Teachers can create exciting, worthwhile activities for children based on this book. Children could investigate ways to conserve the environment. They might develop and implement a plan to encourage others to protect our environment. A classroom could clean up a creek bed and surrounding area. Behind these activities, it is the interconnectedness of the knowledge, skills, and concepts that strengthens children's understanding of the world in which they are a part.

Skill Perspective

Children are expected to gain facility in the science process skills throughout their years in school. Some skills are introduced earlier, such as observing and inferring. Observation is the use of all the senses to gather data about an object or phenomenon. It is the skill that underlies the mastery of all other processes, including inferring, measuring, communicating, and experimenting. A quick glance at the organizers within the strands is a reminder of the strong role literature plays in supporting the development of these skills. Using children's literature to develop these skills provides for a greater emphasis on communication skills, which relate to everything we do. The more complex skills of interpreting, hypothesizing, experimenting, and controlling variables are more appropriately emphasized in the Junior years and beyond. Teachers can use the literature to link with the skills to provide another avenue for developing hands-on learning activities. Teachers can use the *Organizer Chart* within each strand as a model to spring from for their own future planning for various other topics to ensure a balance in teaching the science process skills.

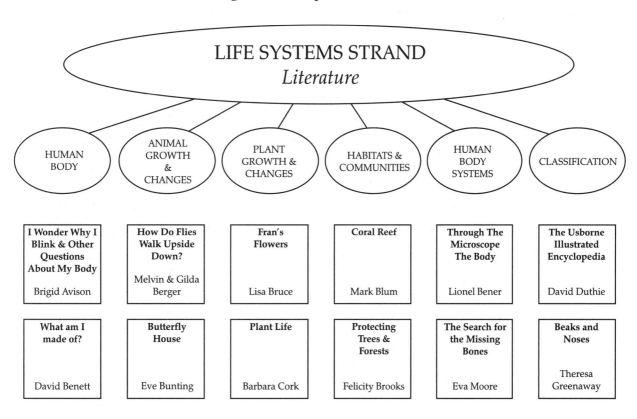

The Role of the Teacher

- Provide classroom opportunities for children to observe and to use all of their senses to acquire information.
- Provide many hands-on activities since the inquiry and design skills must be taught and learned through experiences with concrete materials.

The Role of the Teacher

- Select a learning expectation or group of learning expectations.
- Select books that will help children achieve the learning expectation(s).
- Read a book.
- Make other books that support/reinforce the expectation(s) available to the children.
- Plan hands-on explorations and activities.

Learning Expectation Perspective

The learning expectations provide another angle of sight for implementing science and technology in the classroom. The expectations describe the knowledge and skills that children are expected to develop and to demonstrate. Some of the expectations focus on science and some on technology. Others deal with relating science and technology to each other, to the world outside school, and to the need for sustainable development. Teachers can begin a topic of study with the learning expectations. The learning expectations in *Literature and Science Breakthroughs* are linked to the concepts and key questions. Each strand in this book provides an example of these links to help teachers in their own planning and development of a topic. The first step for using the learning expectations as the angle of sight to implement science and technology is to select a learning expectation or a group of learning expectations that go together within a topic. For example, if children are expected to learn about the Human Body, "parts of the human body" might be the learning expectation. Next, locate a book to introduce the topic and develop hands-on learning activities with equipment and materials, all based on the book. Remember to plan hands-on learning activities so that children can learn concepts through investigation, exploration, observation, and experimentation. Other books identified around the same learning expectation may be used for reinforcement and/or for developing learning activities appropriate to the developmental level of the students.

Concept Perspective

Literature plays an important role in supporting the development of science concepts such as energy, space, time, matter, community, life, change, growth, interrelationships, technology, and conservation. Using broad concepts as your angle of sight, to develop hands-on activities, first, decide whether you want to focus on one concept to strengthen the children's understanding or a multi-set of concepts to reinforce what has already been taught. Next, select the books that focus on the concept(s). Read one of the books to the class to introduce the concept. Finally, develop learning activities that combine science and technology and enable children to develop the communication skills that are an essential component of science and technology education.

Getting Started — A Step-by-Step Process

The Role of the Teacher

- Select a concept for development.
- Use appropriate literature to support planning.
- Provide activities that allow students to discover and learn fundamental concepts through investigations, exploration, observation, and experimentation.
- Place concepts in social, environmental, and economic contexts.

Become familiar with the background and interests of all of your students — talk with them, watch the books they choose, and identify their special areas of interest. Consider the learning styles of the children you teach.

1. Select a science strand and a specific topic within the strand.
2. Use the planning organizer to help you with your planning.
3. Read and select science books on the topic. Refer to the criteria in Chapter Two for selecting good science books.
4. Group the resources and make them accessible to the children. Encourage children to become familiar with the literature.
5. Brainstorm for ideas on the topic cooperatively and develop an integrated web on the topic.
6. Think of potential questions and activities for investigation.
7. Plan activities in partnership with the children, taking into account the research on multiple intelligences and learning styles.
8. Collect the appropriate hands-on equipment and materials.
9. Choose an "angle of sight" to introduce the topic and use appropriate science support books.
10. Have fun watching children *doing* science!

3

Linking the Literature and Hands-on Instruments

A magnifying glass, a pair of binoculars, a periscope — all are among the instruments that teachers might use to encourage children to look more closely at objects. When Albert Einstein was five years old, his father gave him a present: a compass. "Do you see this tiny needle? No matter how you turn the compass, the needle always points to the north." That compass became Einstein's most treasured possession. To Einstein, the compass was not something to play with. He did not look on it as a toy; instead, Einstein saw an instrument that stirred new questions in his mind.

Our role as teacher is to encourage students to progress from one level of understanding and development to the next level. However, children's preconceptions and the explanations they base on them can be deeply rooted and difficult to rout. In one classroom, *Jack and the Beanstalk* was the springboard for an activity in which the children planted their own bean seeds. Each child was given a choice of potting materials for their seeds: sand, soil, or stones. When the children were asked to explain the reasons for their selection, one child believed that stones were best because they would hold the bean plant's roots more firmly. Another child chose sand because it would be a softer landing when you jumped off the beanstalk. These children were at different levels of development, and both firmly believed in their choices. The activity itself would soon demonstrate that bean plants grow differently in different potting materials. Of even greater significance, the children would have a real reason to wonder "Why?"

To facilitate a conceptual change in children, children should be encouraged to explore and ask questions, and they must have the opportunity to interact with materials and instruments appropriate to the learner and the task. According to Foster and Pellens, close observation of students, careful use of questions and answers, and making suggestions to children can help a teacher determine what children are learning from an activity. Because children so often construct their own meaning and make their own sense of the world through their experiences, hands-on materials should be available at all times, to provide several opportunities for children to observe, measure, collect, categorize, record, and interpret data. Literature describes and explains a concept, and hands-on instruments allow children to demonstrate or experience it themselves. By linking literature and instruments in appropriate contexts, we help children develop a stronger understanding of the science concepts and skills.

Linking hands-on instruments with carefully selected books infused with scientific thought invites children to take part in hands-on exploration and investigation. Books can introduce scientific instruments to children in a number of ways: through text and illustrations, instructions for do-it-yourself or homemade instruments and, sometimes, even inclusive devices that come attached to the book.

Method	Scientific Instrument	Literature
Text and illustration	binoculars	*I Spy Treasure Hunt* Jean Marzollo
Inclusive device	3-D StereoFocus Viewer	*Coral Reef* Mark Blum
Do-it-yourself	periscope	*Sound And Light* David Glover

In *I Spy Treasure Hunt* Marzollo uses the text and illustration method to introduce binoculars. The reference is in the text, and children are challenged to explore and discover a pair of binoculars in a treasure chest hidden somewhere in the illustrations in the book. To complete the activity, the book brings a close-up shot of an island into view, demonstrating the use and value of the instrument. When children look at the picture more closely, they will find that the image is placed within a fine lined circle. If you were to look through an actual pair of binoculars, you would not see an object set within a circle; you see the object as well as what surrounds it. Use this information as a teachable moment. Organize children into groups and provide each group with a pair of binoculars. Professionally manufactured binoculars, such as those found in camera or sporting goods stores, can be costly. However, inexpensive pocketsize cardboard binoculars are available, or you could help students make their own. (Instructions for making binoculars can be found in many science activity books.) Direct the children's attention to the picture in the book, and challenge them to discover how the image they see in their binoculars is different from the image produced by manufactured binoculars. Extend their learning with a field trip in the school yard, where children can use binoculars to make their observations and draw what they see in their science journals. Ask students where else they have seen binoculars, how they were used, and who was using them. Encourage the children to explain why binoculars are important to the people who use them on a regular basis.

I highly recommend searching for science books that come with the instrument attached. It is almost a guarantee that children will use these inclusive devices. Mark Blum's *Coral Reef* includes a 3-D StereoFocus Viewer and a set of twenty-four stereographic (3-D) cards. Directions are included, showing the user how to view the 3-D cards. The viewer is very durable, easy to use, and is easily detached from the book, making it easy for children to use. Children are given opportunities to go eye-to-eye with an octopus, hermit crab, scorpion fish, sharks, (and more) with the viewer and this set of cards. What better way to draw children into the exciting world of science than by providing a hands-on instrument that is fun to use at the same time it strengthens their observation skills.

The do-it-yourself method has been around for decades. With a little effort, children can make a science instrument to match anyone's fancy. This tried and true method uses a variety of materials, often recyclable objects, to make science instruments. At low or no cost, a classroom can be filled with plenty of easily accessible instruments. This method not only eases a teacher's financial burden, but also teaches children to be stewards of our environment by using the four Rs: Reduce, Reuse, Recycle, and Refuse. Children also become active partners in collecting and organizing the necessary materials as well as making the actual instruments. The result is a sense of great pride in their work. In *Sound And Light*, a book selected for the Energy and Control Strand, David Glover uses a cardboard carton and two mirrors of the same size to make a periscope. Children follow four easy steps to make the instrument, and color pictures in the book demonstrate its appropriate use.

The science books recommended in *Literature and Science Breakthroughs* have been carefully chosen to represent these three methods for bringing science instruments into the classroom and ensuring that children will have plenty of opportunities to explore, discover, and investigate in a hands-on learning environment. An example of one recommended title and its related instrument for each of the five strands is provided below to illustrate how hands-on instruments can be used with text and illustrations in the classroom.

• Life Systems

In *Usborne's Mysteries and Marvels of Plant Life,* Cork provides enlarged images of plants and seeds throughout the book, reflecting the use and function of magnifiers in science. Using this book, children are compelled to examine the mysteries of plants and to uncover new and interesting concepts about them. In the classroom, provide the children with magnifiers. Ask them to think about the pictures in the book, and what it means to magnify an object. Then provide the children with a variety of items that they can view through their magnifiers to hone their observation skills.

• Matter and Materials

Text and illustrations support the explanation of the use and function of a thermometer as a measurement instrument found in *The Usborne*

Illustrated Encyclopedia — Science and Technology. Children learn that measurement instruments are used regularly in science to determine accuracy, one of the habits of mind a scientist requires to validate data.

• Energy and Control
David Glover's book *Sound And Light* introduces new vocabulary terms, such as concave and convex. A pocket magnifier is used to demonstrate and explain how concave and convex lenses are used in eye glasses. Scientific terminology and language used within the text alongside the hands-on use of the instrument helps children to strengthen their understanding. To extend the learning, invite children to reflect on where and how convex and concave lenses are used outside the school.

• Structures and Mechanisms
The Carousel, by Liz Rosenberg and illustrated by Jim LaMarche, is an excellent demonstration of how curiosity is a crucial habit of mind in science. One wonderful illustration is of a girl surrounded with tools and pulleys, gears, and wheels and axles. The mechanisms are parts of a broken carousel that the girl willingly and diligently sets out to repair. Rosenberg's text uses vocabulary associated with the use of tools such as a wrench, a screwdriver, and a pair of needle-nosed pliers. The storyline cements the link between literature and hands-on experiences. It clearly sets the stage and inspires students for projects where they design and build their own working models.

• Earth and Space Science
Opportunities for hands-on exploration and discovery are inherent in this strand. Joanna Cole's *The Magic School Bus Inside the Earth* role models various ways to actively participate in the study of rocks and fossils. Equipment and scientific instruments, for example, rock hammer, rock grinder, drill, shovel, hand lens, and fossil and rock specimens, are interwoven throughout the text and illustrations. Encourage students to begin their own rock collection as a follow up to this book.

The task of organizing your classroom to effectively link children's literature with hands-on instruments may seem overwhelming, but it can be handled simply. Obtain a mobile cart with sufficient space for the literature and the hands-on equipment. Store manipulative items in deep-sided containers, or in tubs. The first three shelves can hold the individual containers or tubs, and the bottom shelf can be used to store the relevant literature about the hands-on equipment. If your classroom is not set up for this kind of storage system, you may be able to use one of the ones described below.

• Window Sill Science Centers
Kepler suggests turning the classroom window sill into a lab for easy-to-do science investigations. Create Window Sill Science Centers, complete with the equipment and how-to-use instructions, by combining and storing the hands-on materials with the related science literature.

• Science Boxes

Obtain several boxes of the same size (to fit your *largest* item), and develop different Science Boxes. The boxes hold the related literature and the hands-on equipment. You and the students should have easy access to the Science Boxes for science experiences on an ongoing basis.

• Sealable Science Bags

Re-sealable bags come in a variety of sizes and weights/strengths, and are good for storing many hands-on items. If the bags are not large enough to hold the relevant literature choices, include a list of titles that children can use with the manipulatives in the bag.

• Lunch Pail Buckets

I have tried this method with my class. Each student brought in an old lunch pail that had a spot for a thermos. In the beginning of the year, we discussed what kinds of science instruments they might want to use during the year. For Outdoor Studies, we set up Young Biologist Groups, and filled some lunch pails with items such as hand lenses, bug box magnifiers, and so on. We also included field guides, such as *Peterson's First Guides — Insects,* by John C. Kricher, as part of the literature that students could take out into the field.

To help you identify instruments and specific books related to them, *Literature and Science Breakthroughs* includes a topic organizer for the topic explored in each strand. This topic organizer shows you at a glance what concepts, skills, and hands-on instruments, materials, and equipment are introduced in each book for the topic. It can be helpful to consider the actual hands-on experience called for in each piece of literature so that children are assured opportunities to explore, investigate, and discover in a variety of ways.

No matter which of these methods you choose, the bottom line is to ensure that children are doing science, using hands-on instruments and appropriate literature references and support.

4

Linking Science, Assessment Techniques, and Evaluation

Assessment Provides Data

Assessment is the process of continuously gathering information about student learning and performance using a variety of sources, for example, projects, that accurately reflects how well a student is achieving the learning expectations.

Evaluation Brings Meaning to the Data

Evaluation refers to the process of judging the quality of student work with assessments on the basis of established criteria, as in rubrics, and assigning a value to represent the quality of how each criterion was met.

Assessment and evaluation address both the processes and products of student work. *How* students work is the process, and the products that children produce are things such as posters, timelines, dioramas, scale drawings, mobiles, and so on. The purpose of assessment and evaluation is to improve student learning. Assessment is a continuous process involving listening, observing, and asking questions to promote intellectual growth.

Assessment guides instruction and instruction guides assessment. Teachers should match the assessment techniques with the style of instruction and learning. New methods of assessment allow teachers to evaluate children's conceptual development and their process skills and problem-solving abilities.

Implementing a good science program requires the use of a broad range of assessment techniques. *Literature and Science Breakthroughs* integrates many assessment techniques with the suggested hands-on activities. Through using each type of assessment technique, teachers will become familiar with its strengths, efficiency, and appropriateness and will be able to select the assessment technique(s) that will work best for a particular situation.

Teachers must be aware of, and adapt to, the broad range of students in a class. It's possible that as many as half the students in a single class will require program modifications. Research about students' learning styles and multiple kinds of intelligence indicates that no one form of assessment can possibly fit each individual student's needs because every student learns and performs differently — even from one time to another.

In any science program, it is critical to develop items that assess the science ideas children are learning, and the children's conceptual understanding and ability to use science skills and processes. "How can I assess hands-on activities?" is a common question asked by teachers who are planning their science program. Hands-on experiences allow for a more varied approach to assessment. The key is to assess students' knowledge and skills in a variety of different situations using a variety of assessment techniques. Techniques such as checklists, anecdotal notes, or performance tasks allow teachers to record students' actions and responses while they are working at an activity. However, choosing which assessment strategy to use can be difficult without guidelines.

This chapter will assist teachers in ensuring a balance among the assessment techniques available within a hands-on activity-based science program. *Literature and Science Breakthroughs* suggests teachers share with their students the purpose of the task, the method, and how the assignment is to be evaluated prior to engaging students in the task. By identifying the expectations for each unit ahead of time, teachers can work back in order to plan their teaching. Pre-planning the assessment activities and techniques that will be used with the students will also help to ensure adequate demonstration of their learning.

The focus is always on what the student has achieved in relation to the learning expectations and on how that achievement has been demonstrated.

The systematic integration of assessment, process and product.

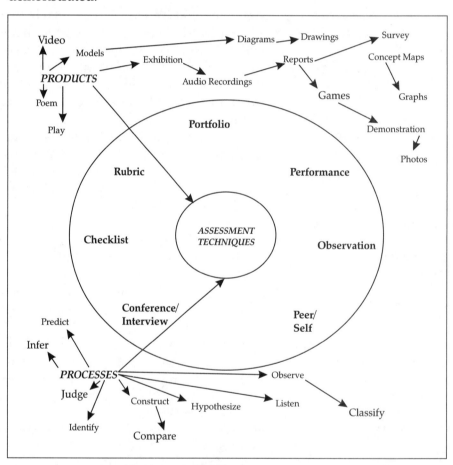

In my Grade 4 class, more than half of the children were special needs students. Many students were unable to read or write at grade level, a few students performed at the upper grade level, and the remainder of the students were at grade level. The biggest challenge I faced was to find a fair way of assessing all students.

The next step is identifying an instructional approach to ensure learning opportunities for all students. With a diverse group of students, the literature-based approach to teaching science can be extremely useful. Hands-on science activities developed from the literature can provide children with concrete experiences for developing a foundation for learning more abstract concepts. For example, students can learn about

The Role of the Teacher

- Note the concepts and skills you expect the students to know, to do, and to apply.
- Select assessment techniques that incorporate the learning styles of your students.
- Choose assessment techniques that directly relate to the activities.

The Role of the Student

- Monitor progress.
- Reflect on learning.
- Evaluate understanding.

structures by creating models with toothpicks, straws, pipe cleaners, marshmallows, and a host of other hands-on equipment and materials. Students with different learning styles or aspects of multiple intelligences are able to grasp the same scientific concepts when they are introduced to them in trade books that match their learning patterns and areas of interest.

Consider a lesson on the use and function of the microscope. It is easily presented through a combination of appropriate literature and experience with the hands-on equipment. In the pre-planning stage, the teacher might set the expectation that at the end of the lesson, each student would know how to use a microscope. Students could work in small groups to complete the assigned task. Following the exploratory stage the children might work cooperatively to grasp the fundamental understanding that using a microscope increases their ability to observe and results in a greater degree of accuracy. The student groups could also be involved in deciding how their group wants to be assessed, and accommodations could be made for that kind of assessment to take place. By combining the literature, hands-on activity, and a variety of student-centered assessment techniques, such as journals, portfolios, peer and self evaluation, and interviews, teachers can ensure that all students have the opportunity to succeed.

A Sampler of Assessment Techniques and Tools

Assessment Technique: Science Journals

Insight

The Science Journal provides students with the opportunity to express their thoughts, ideas, and even questions all in one place. Students write statements in their journals that address what they learned, what they do not understand, what else they would like to know. Their Journal may include key issues and concerns. It can be as simple as a student notebook, take on an elaborate shape, or be as topic specific as you would like it to be (for example, a Geologist's Journal).

Use

- As a log for describing experimental procedures, observations, and conclusions
- As a record of children's growth in thinking, reflecting children's conceptual understandings and attitudes

Purpose

- To provide the opportunity for children to demonstrate their science and technology learning
- To offer an avenue for students to reflect upon their learning
- To provide an opportunity for students to use scientific language when communicating

Characteristics

- May contain a record of student observations, data, results of experiments, drawings, written notes, procedures and results from investigations, hypotheses, inferences about scientific phenomena, questions, an evaluation of a lesson, measurements, and so forth
- May have a specific set of sub-criteria for how each type of entry should be included
- May form the basis of a student portfolio

Advantage

- Provides an opportunity to assess ongoing changes in children's understandings and thinking
- Identifies misconceptions
- Provides proof of student learning and growth for parent/teacher conferences

Assessment Link

Science Journals can be assessed on a formal and/or informal basis. Assess children's Science Journals based on the criteria you and the children set. You can use a rubric to effectively assess student journals and look for indicators of their understanding, their level of interest in a topic, or their comprehension of related skills.

Educators continue to find innovative ways to evaluate children's progress using the Science Journal. This can be done quite simply by providing a context for the children's entries in their journals. Investigating solids and liquids offers opportunities for children to compare and contrast different samples of materials, or to describe their experience with different liquids. Different structures observed on a field trip could be recorded. The children might explain what they already know about magnets and where they have seen them used. The teacher can take the children's entries and check on their observation skills, ability to follow directions for an activity, their understanding of what they observed, or perhaps their preconceptions about a topic.

Implementing Science Journals in the Classroom

Students may keep science journals for each of the topics they study during the year. Introduce the concept of the Science Journal to the children by sharing some books, such as *A Flower Grows* by Ken Robbins, or *Somewhere In The World Right Now* by Stacey Schuett, that illustrate the passage of time. Discuss the value of keeping a record of events to reflect upon later. Discuss the components of a Science Journal: data that is gathered during an activity, drawings to illustrate a concept, or a story to describe something they learned. *The Inventor's Diary* by Jane Buxton provides an example of data that students may want to include in their Science Journals.

Work with the children to set assessment criteria that include "habits of mind" as well as knowledge and understanding. Make a list of the indicators that demonstrate the makings of a good Science Journal and post it on the classroom wall for children to refer to. Encourage children to use their Science Journal, and have them share their entries in a large group setting. Use Science Journals regularly as one method of assessing children's knowledge, skills, and attitudes.

I used Science Journals on a regular basis. When my Grade 4 class was studying a unit on insects, we prepared to observe insects in the school yard. I cut notebooks in two to make reasonably sized Science Journals for my students. We called our journals a special name: *Insectopedia Journal*. Students carried their journal inside old lunch pails, which also held their special magnifiers and insect field guides. They used their journals to note each insect and the location where it was sighted. Back in the classroom, the students wrote about their experience in their *Insectopedia Journals* and included a fully labeled insect diagram of their favorite sighting.

Assessment Technique: Portfolios

Insight

The Portfolio contains a purposeful collection of samples of each student's work that shows progress, improvement, and significant learning. The Portfolio should include items that the student feels represent his/her best work. The Portfolio consists of student products that may include things like drawings, projects, photographs, or diagrams. The teacher and students work together to devise a method for storing the work samples, such as a home-made folder, box, album, or duotang. Teachers can create a form for students to fill out and place in their storage container when video tapes or other such media devices or models are the means used to demonstrate student learning.

Use
- As a means to monitor student progress
- To teach children to reflect on what they have learned
- To set goals for future improvement

Purpose
- To provide ongoing records of student performance
- To help students develop techniques such as self-evaluation in assessing their own work
- To monitor growth of the student's knowledge, skills, and attitudes
- To allow the student to express his/her learning in a variety of ways

Characteristics
- Includes concrete examples of the student's work
- Provides opportunities for student/teacher/parent conferences
- Allows for students with different learning styles
- Shows evidence of student self-reflection

Advantage

- Provides significant evidence of student progress
- Allows students to be central to the process
- Encourages active, self-directed learning
- Provides opportunities for students to take ownership of their work
- Offers a long-term record of student achievement
- Encourages individual and group collaboration
- Encourages effective written and oral communication

Assessment Link

Evaluation of Portfolios varies according to the objectives of the Portfolio assignment. Many elementary teachers have found innovative ways to evaluate children's progress in science by using the Portfolio.

Students who don't have the facility to read and write well can opt to put their collection in the Portfolio as part of their overall assessment. What we have to remember when using the Portfolio for assessment, however, is to carefully identify the material that shows evidence of process, product, and interaction.

Implementing Portfolios in the Classroom

The organizational work around implementing Portfolios as an assessment technique in the classroom needs to be in place before introducing the concept to the students. Questions such as, "What should I expect students to include in the Portfolio? How will it be used? How and where will it be stored?" need to be addressed by the teacher as part of the pre-planning process. I used portfolios for assessment in my Grade 4 class. I explained to the students that their projects were to be compiled in a container of their choice for a Portfolio assessment. After some discussion, the students were interested in making a home-made folder for their samples of work. We agreed on a place to store the folders, set the criteria for selection of work samples, and discussed how they might play a role in deciding the indicators to be used for evaluation of their work. In our conversations, we also discussed how we might include large products for assessment — even though they did not fit in the physical space of the container. Our first unit of study was Structures. Students chose to represent their learning in a variety of ways. Some built free-standing structures, while others chose to show their learning by doing an experiment. Students took photos with the class Polaroid camera and included them in their Portfolio as part of the material for assessment.

Assessment Technique: Rubrics

Insight

A Rubric allows teachers, students, and parents to be partners in the assessment process. It is an assessment technique that describes the criteria by which a student product, performance, or demonstration will be assessed. It serves a dual purpose: When properly constructed, it can guide and improve instruction, while it also serves as an assessment technique. Rubrics outline and define levels of achievement and quality work related to a specific task or set of tasks. The success of the Rubric rests on how clearly the rubric communicates the expected criteria for achievement to students and parents.

Use

- As an assessment technique, the Rubric provides students with a clear idea of what they are doing well, what they need to work at more, and what the next steps are for improving
- As an assessment technique, it helps enhance student performance by defining the criteria of specific achievement

Purpose

- To define standards for students and parents
- To provide clear criteria on achievement for students
- To promote and improve student self-assessment
- To assist children in understanding the learning expectations and how they might improve the quality of their work

Characteristics

- Reveals a strong high-quality assessment process
- Allows students to see what went well and what didn't
- Incorporates score sheets that spell out how a project, performance, or a response will be marked
- Encourages collaboration between and among colleagues with the same grade level

Advantage

- Provides teachers with a strong assessment tool for discussing with parents/guardians the basis of the grades they assign to students
- Improves student learning
- Involves students in the assessment process because they help to build the Rubric
- Makes assessing student work quick and efficient

Linking Science and Assessment

A Rubric is an authentic approach to assessment. Teachers of elementary science have waited a long time for an assessment technique that could be used in science teaching and learning to serve both instructional and assessment needs. When students involve themselves in hands-on learning activities, as they do in science, they are eager to know how well they are doing and how they can improve their learning. Using a Rubric as a means to evaluate science teaching and learning — for example, criteria to identify expectations on how specific science equipment is used or criteria about expectations for students working with others to do a science experiment — can only help to improve our students' understanding of science. Teachers are encouraged to use the four levels of achievement as points of reference in reviewing and determining how well students are achieving the expectations set for a specific area of study. The levels of achievement also provide students with clear authentic guidelines when they receive feedback on how well they have learned the knowledge, skills, and concepts set out in the criteria in the Rubric. Using this information provides students with ongoing opportunities to improve upon their learning.

Implementing Rubrics in the Science Classroom

The pre-planning stage is important in implementing Rubrics as an assessment technique in science teaching and learning. The key to success is to communicate a clear message to students and parents alike. Many teachers, children, and parents/guardians find it useful to discuss questions such as "What is a rubric? How will it be used? What place does it have in the science program?" Students want to know how they can become a full partner in the learning process. When the true purpose is shared with the students, they feel at ease and become great contributors in the development and implementation of Rubrics in the science classroom. Parents, too, are interested in knowing how their child will be evaluated. Taking time in the initial stages of implementation to explain these things to students and their parents/guardians is well worth it.

Recently I had the pleasure of observing a Rubric at work in a Grade 2 classroom at my school. I observed the teacher outline the task in which the children would be participating. They were beginning a science unit on Wind and Water. Their task was to design a wind- or water-powered device. As part of the planning, the teacher involved the children in a brainstorming exercise to determine the criteria for assessment. Prior to this unit of study, the students had lots of time to work with setting criteria and choosing appropriate indicators of success. Students were taught how to apply the Rubric to the task. When students completed their models of the devices, they gathered around the teacher. The teacher reviewed the criteria and the corresponding indicators. Students were encouraged to judge the models based on a four-point scale. There was a lot of dialogue going on when the actual assessment was taking place. When consensus was achieved in assessing each model, the teacher used the rubric to record the children's results. This was a rewarding experience. Students not only received a mark, they knew how they could improve for their next creation.

Technique: Peer- and Self-Assessment

Insight

Peer- and self-assessment play a significant role in the learning process in any science classroom. For example, when students are required to select materials to include in their Portfolios they naturally reflect on their own learning. This act of reflection is an integral component of self-assessment. On the other hand, peer-assessment occurs when a student's work is evaluated by other students in the class. Very often these techniques are already at work in the elementary science classroom. Students are afforded multiple opportunities to practice peer- and self-assessment strategies. A variety of checklists are available to help students gain facility in the use of this double-sided technique. Such checklists serve as a guide for students in the use of this strategy. Some schools have a science buddy program where students routinely and regularly share the procedure and results of experiments they conduct. As well, students are paired up frequently to work on investigations inside and outside the school. Field trips offer further opportunity for students to demonstrate the skills inherent in peer-and self-assessment, as the children are often assigned to groups with specific tasks to accomplish on the outing.

Use
- Provides opportunities for students to assess themselves and others
- Promotes both peer- and self-assessment as an ongoing part of a balanced assessment program

Purpose
- To encourage students to take on more responsibility for their learning
- To encourage students to become increasingly aware of their own strengths, weaknesses, and attitudes
- To encourage students to provide useful feedback to the other person
- To enhance self-esteem

Characteristics
- Self-assessment is an essential component of formative assessment
- Students are engaged to develop their own learning criteria
- Students are encouraged to take on more responsibility for their own learning

Advantage
- Students learn to take risks
- Students grow to understand their own attitudes, skills, and knowledge

Linking Science and Assessment
Students can assess themselves and others in science only when they have a clear picture of the target expectations for their learning. Teachers need to share the learning expectations for a unit of study with all students. It is important to set aside a large time-block so that students can question and discuss anything they need to find out more about. Provide the children with any checklists of indicators/descriptors that you and your students should use for a given unit, project, activity, or lesson. These provide a sense of direction. Checklists can also serve as a guide for students when they are assessing their own work and the work of others.

Implementing Peer- and Self-assessment in the Science Classroom

The role of the teacher in establishing peer- and self-assessment in the science classroom is to develop students' skills in assessing and connecting their own work according to the expectations. It is truly rewarding for both students and the teacher when students feel comfortable enough to incorporate peer- and self-evaluation strategies. For this strategy to be effective, students must have the necessary skills, and teachers should teach these to students if they are not already familiar with them.

In my Grade 6 class, the students were given a task to work on with their science buddy. One student elected to make a science instrument to be used to teach about balance. The two buddies worked together to construct the apparatus. They wrote down the directions for making the instrument and set about putting together a plan to share this new piece of equipment. Their idea was to use this piece of equipment to teach the concept of balance to students in Grade 1. Before taking the idea into unknown territory, they asked for feedback from their peers. Following that, they were ready to accept the challenge. They created a simple picture questionnaire to involve the little guys in the evaluation process.

Technique: Performance-Based Assessment

Insight

Performance-based Assessment is an ongoing process that involves giving one or more students a task that will enable teachers to see not only an answer, but also the process used to find that answer. Performance-based Assessment allows students to demonstrate the skills and knowledge they have gained through doing the activities.

Use

- Effective in assessing process skills and problem-solving abilities
- Provides teachers with information about how the student understands and applies knowledge

Purpose

- To encourage learners to demonstrate abilities, skills, and attitudes
- To evaluate practical skills and application of techniques
- Allows for the evaluation of both process and product
- Addresses all types of student evaluation — Diagnostic, Formative, and Summative

Characteristics

- Enables students to rise to their highest performance levels
- Encourages ongoing feedback

Advantage
- Portrays a real-life connection
- Allows students to formulate their own ideas and questions
- Accommodates special needs students through an alternative assessment method

Linking Science and Assessment

Performance-based Assessment provides the means for evaluating the scientific processes and the skills related to organizing and presenting information. Science Fair projects, Learning Kits, and Exhibitions, in which students display their work and talk about the development process of their project, all require that students know, understand, and apply organizational and presentation skills. The Performance-based Assessment technique provides children with the opportunity to demonstrate their mastery of science process skills.

In my Grade 6 classroom students worked in pairs to invent a product. Part of their assignment was to establish criteria for evaluating their project and to create a marketing plan for their product. A group of two students developed a software package about "Light." They worked together on a significant presentation to launch their software. It resulted in an engagement at one of the very large hotels in Toronto. From process to product, these students demonstrated a high degree of organizational and presentation skills. A checklist of the criteria was used to assess their project. This was a real-life application experience for these two students, linking science with assessment.

Implementing Performance-based Assessment in the Science Classroom

Performance-based Assessment techniques have great opportunities for application in the classroom. The first step in implementing this technique is for teachers to determine the activity and the task to be assessed in that activity.

Drama is a comprehensive Performance-based Assessment opportunity. It allows teachers to observe the meaning children have constructed while the learning was taking place. If misconceptions are apparent as children act out a concept, the teacher can help students identify and correct them. (Detailed information about this type of Performance Assessment can be found in "Performance Assessment: Five Practical Approaches," Anne Grall Reichel. *Science and Children,* October 1994).

My Grade 4 students put on mini-drama plays, linking literature and science for a study of water. As a large group my class developed the criteria to be used for evaluation purposes. The evaluation started in the initial stages of planning the project. It consisted of developing a checklist. Students then performed in small groups. Feedback included dialogue around the qualities of their work, with advice on how they could improve it.

The Ultimate Goal of Assessment

Through the use of these and other assessment techniques, we can help all students to succeed in communicating their knowledge of science content and science processes, both within school and in the world outside of school. My hope is for assessment techniques to continue to move in the direction of student involvement — both physically and mentally — in the learning process. "It's time for new assessment in science education. To do science, children must interact with the physical world — drop objects, observe butterfly larvae, measure length and speed, build electric circuits and test them — and they must participate in the world of ideas — design experiments, test theories, hypothesize, predict, discuss, and argue." (*Active Assessment for Active Science* by George Hein and Sabra Price. (Heinemann, 1995).

Literature and Science Breakthroughs provides numerous opportunities for children to do science and use technology in the five science strands developed in Chapter 5. We can use innovative assessment techniques such as video quizzes, mini-plays based on conceptual development from the books, rubrics for advertisements the children develop to promote their own assessment products. When we open ourselves to using new assessment tools and techniques, we role-model the very habits of mind we want our students to demonstrate.

Recommended Professional Resources

1. *Science Assessment* by Julia Jasmine. Grade 5/6. 1994
2. *Science Assessment* by Julia Jasmine. Grade 1/2. 1994
3. *Science Assessment* by Julia Jasmine. Grade 3/4. 1994
4. *Early Childhood Assessment* by Julia Jasmine. 1995
5. *Student Self-Assessment* by Graham Foster. 1996 Pembroke
6. *Hitting The Mark: Assessment Tools For Teachers* by Don Aker. 1995 Pembroke
7. *Marking Success: A Guide to Evaluation for Teachers of English* by Neil Graham & Jerry George. 1992 Pembroke
8. *Learning To See: Assessment through Observation* by Mary Jane Drummond. 1994 Pembroke
9. *Observing Children* by Doreen Norris and Joyce Boucher. The Board of Education for the City of Toronto
10. *Active Assessment for Active Science: A Guide for Elementary School Teachers* by G. E. Hein and P. Sabra. 1994 Heinemann
11. *Classroom Teacher Developed Assessments* by P. Montoya. 1994 Mesa Public Schools Arizona
12. *Pan-Canadian Science Place — Program & Assessment Guide*. 2000 Scholastic Canada Ltd.

5

The Five Strands

Life Systems Strand

The Life Systems strand combines the study of traditional topics in life science with technology as it relates to basic human needs.

Literature and Science Breakthroughs uses a literature-based approach to teaching the Life Systems strand, linking children's literature with science concepts and skills. Many teachers have a strong language arts background, and the literature-based approach to science in this book uses their strength in language to good advantage. Ten science books of varying genres, for example, story, novel, verse, are suggested for each topic of study. Organizers such as webs and charts are included in the book to save teachers time in planning and to help them plan more effectively to ensure the children are involved in doing science. These organizers provide an overview of the topics and the recommended books. The ultimate goal is to move all children towards achieving the learning expectations through the use of the books that lead to hands-on discovery, exploration, and investigation activities.

Each topic is introduced by a summary. The topic organizer that identifies the books is noted in the margin. The learning expectations for the entire topic are provided after the summary. Each topic is then broken down into a scaffolded sequence of Key Questions. Within each strand two Key Questions for each topic are developed. For example, in the Life Systems strand two Key Questions from Animal Growth and Changes are explored leading to opportunities for further cooperative planning and development of the topic by teachers and children in the classroom. The Key Questions evolve from the specific Key Concepts to be developed within the topic and build on what the children have just learned, while narrowing their focus within a given topic. Every Key Question includes Learning Expectations, Key Concepts, Teaching Outline, Planning Web, Hands-on Activities, and Evaluation Strategies to help teachers identify how the children will meet the expectations for science concepts and skills through exploration.

LIFE SYSTEMS STRAND
Literature

HUMAN BODY	ANIMAL GROWTH & CHANGES	PLANT GROWTH & CHANGES	HABITATS & COMMUNITIES	HUMAN BODY SYSTEMS	CLASSIFICATION
I Wonder Why I Blink & Other Questions About My Body — Brigid Avison	How Do Flies Walk Upside Down? — Melvin & Gilda Berger	Fran's Flowers — Lisa Bruce	Coral Reef — Mark Blum	Through The Microscope The Body — Lionel Bener	The Usborne Illustrated Encyclopedia — David Duthie
What Am I Made Of? — David Benett	Butterfly House — Eve Bunting	Plant Life — Barbara Cork	Protecting Trees & Forests — Felicity Brooks	The Search for the Missing Bones — Eva Moore	Beaks and Noses — Theresa Greenaway
What's He Doing Now? — Patti Farm	The Magic School Bus Inside a Beehive — Joanna Cole	Mouse & Mole and the Year Round Garden — Doug Cushman	Where Once There Was a Wood — Denise Fleming	Creatures, Features & Funny Bones — Anita Ganer	Wings, Stings & Wriggly Things — Martin Jenkins
Body Detectives — Elroy Freem	Where Are The Night Animals? — Mary Ann Fraser	From Seed to Plant — Gail Gibbons	Walk With a Wolf — Janni Hawker	You and Your Body — Sally Hewitt	Eyewitness Books Insects — Laurence Mound
It's Science Growing Up — Sally Hewitt	The Best Book of Bugs — Claire Llewellyn	What Shall I Grow? — Ray Gibson	It's Science All Kinds of Habitats — Sally Hewitt	Watch Me Grow — Michelle Palmer	Have You Seen Bugs? — Joanne Oppenheim & Ron Broda
Oxford First Encyclopedia My Body — Andrew Langley	Have You Seen Bugs? — Joanne Oppenheim & Ron Broda	Ladybug Garden — Celia Godkin	Habitats — Pamela Hickman	The Heart and Blood — Steve Parker	The Giant Book of Snakes and Slithery Creatures — Jim Pipe
The Bone Keeper — Megan McDonald	Frogs & Toads — Ellen Schultz	Ben Plants a Butterfly Garden — Kate Petty	Animal Hide & Seek — Andrew Langley	Steven Biesty's Incredible Body — Richard Platt	3-D Bees & Micro Fleas — Shar Levine, Dr. Elaine Humphrey, Leslie Johnstone
The Search For The Missing Bones — Eva Moore	Exploding Ants: Amazing Facts About How Animals Adapt — Joanne Settel	The Gardener — Sarah Stewart	Wetlands Nature Search — Andrew Langley	Muscles — Seymour Simon	Micro Aliens Dazzling Journey with an Electron Microscope — Howard Tomb & Dennis Kunkel
How Have I Grown? — Mary Reid	The Barn Owl — Sally Tagholm	Flowers, Trees & Other Plants — John Stidworthy	Our Mysterious Ocean — Peter Riley	Me and My Amazing Body — Joan Sweeney	Bizarre Birds — Doug Wechsler
The Amazing Pull-out, Pop-up Body in a Book — Pennie Smith Caroline Bingham	Bugs & Slugs — Judy Tatchell	June 29, 1999 — David Weisner	The Natural World in the Rainforest — Barbara Taylor	Earthlings Inside and Out — Valerie Wyatt	Spiders Spin Webs — Yvonne Winer

Biologists' Study Leads to New Technology

Biologists in one study have been observing the characteristics of freshly dead geckos for decades. When looped through the air towards a plate of glass, freshly dead geckos stick to the glass. These research biologists have used their observations of dead geckos to develop the means for measuring the actual adhesive force. In turn, this adhesive force may lead engineers to develop a self-cleaning sticky pad that would work in a vacuum.

Fish Organs Lead to Submarines

Most fish have an organ called a swim bladder (air bladder). This organ contains a mixture of air and water. The fish's depth in water depends on how much air is inside the sac. As the amount of air decreases the fish sinks lower. As the amount of air increases the fish rises closer to the surface. This depth control structure has been adapted in the submarine allowing the submarines' crew to adjust its depth.

Topic Organizer

Animal Growth and Changes provides an overview of ten science books that focus on the topic. See page 59.

Teachers can use the reproducible: *Template for Organizing Books* to develop the remaining topics in the Life Systems strand, for example, Plant Growth and Changes.

Many children react to insects by wanting to step on them. The study of Life Systems emphasizes a love of nature and gives children the opportunity to investigate interactions between living things and their environment. David Suzuki said, "The most important thing we can do is to teach children to love nature." The love of nature, he contends, is the key to producing a generation that is concerned about the environment and interested in science.

The Life Systems strand focuses on six topics: Human Body, Human Body Systems, Animal Growth and Changes, Plant Growth and Changes, Habitats and Communities, and Classification. It is expected that through the study of Life Systems children will understand the basic concepts of life science and will develop skills of inquiry, design, and communication. Children will also learn to relate science and technology to the world outside school. This is particularly important in life science since we very often look to nature to help us find new solutions to issues, concerns and/or problems—are old and long-standing or brand new.

Topic Summary: Animal Growth and Changes

Animals of all sizes and kinds fascinate children, who eagerly use their senses to find out all they can about the creatures. Children are innately curious and usually want to learn all about the animals they encounter. For example, my grandchildren adopted a hedgehog for a family pet which they named, Cedar. They have all kinds of questions about the care of their new pet. I take great pleasure in watching them observe Cedar's behavior. They have discovered that he groans when he is unhappy, and rolls himself in a ball, revealing his very prickly quills, when he feels threatened. Chances are the children's own curiosity will encourage them to ask and learn more about Cedar's life processes — what he likes to eat, his sleeping pattern, how he stays clean, and so on. Children are innately curious and have a need to ask questions about these creatures.

Teachers can encourage all children's eagerness to learn by providing a risk-free environment that is open to inquiry and investigation opportunities.

KEY CONCEPT	LEARNING EXPECTATIONS
• There are many kinds of animals.	• Characteristics of animal groups
	• Group/classify animals
KEY QUESTION 1	• Observe the life process of an animal
• What is an insect?	

Learning Expectations for the Topic

- Characteristics of animal groups
- Group/classify animals
- Changes over time
- Effects of humans on environment
- Effects of seasons on animals
- Observe the life process of an animal

Teaching Outline

- Step One Record all the things students know about insects.
- Step Two List questions students still have about insects.
- Step Three Read *James and the Giant Peach.*
- Step Four Discuss the ideas put forth in the book.
- Step Five Develop a cooperative web incorporating the thoughts and ideas from the book.
- Step Six Plan activities to extend the students' learning.

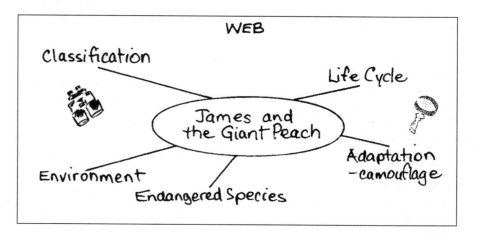

Motivator

Read aloud *James and the Giant Peach* by Roald Dahl. In this novel Roald Dahl captivates our interest in insects through rich, descriptive language complemented by powerful black and white sketches. Immediately, children are drawn to learning more about insects through the magic of story. Concepts covered in the novel include:

- There are many kinds of insects.
- Insects adapt to their environment.
- Some insects are helpful and some are harmful.

Hands-on Activities

The learning and evaluation procedures in terms of expectations should be clearly understood before children begin.

1. Demonstrate how to catch insects. Ask children to collect and observe insects in containers, such as nets, midispectors, and bug boxes. Have

children use a field guide to help them identify the insects. Using these guides shows children that they can learn about the environment from books. Ask children to make their own insect guide for insects they collected. Children draw a picture of each insect they collected and print the name of the insect below their drawing. Children return the insects to the outdoors when the investigation is complete, teaching children to be compassionate and respectful of all life.

2. Display great science books for children to use as a reference. *The Science of Living Things How do Animals Adapt?* by Bobbie Kalman makes an excellent addition to any classroom library. Take the children on an observation excursion. Ask children to observe the many ways in which insects adapt to their environment. They choose one insect and make a diorama showing its adaptation feature(s). Display the student dioramas in the library for others to learn about how insects adapt to their environment.

3. Have children use magnifiers to make first hand observations of insects in their environments. They make a papier-maché model of an insect of their choice noting the specific characteristics of their insect. Ask children to share their findings with a friend. Make insect models into insectopedia mobiles to brighten the classroom environment.

4. Some insects are called noise makers (for example, crickets). Have available *The Very Quiet Cricket* by Eric Carle to motivate children to look for other insect noise makers. Play an audio tape of sounds insects make. Children look at a collection of insects or photographs of insects and identify the noise makers they heard on the tape.

5. Display all resource books on ants. Be sure to include *Ants* by Trevor Terry and Margaret Linton. I managed to see it in my grandson's home library. The illustrations are very large and colorful. The vocabulary is easily understood in the context of story. Have children do research about how to make an ant village. Invite children to make their own live ant village and observe the activities of ants carefully as they build and maintain a network of tunnels. Ask children to record their observations in their Anthology Science Journals. Encourage the use of magnifying lenses to observe the behavior of ants.

Assessment

Book: *James and the Giant Peach*	Rubric	Portfolio	Performance	Journal	Checklist	Observation	Conference	Peer/ Self
Insect Guide			✔					
Diorama	✔							
Mobile						✔		
Listening					✔			
Observing Ant Behaviour				✔				

KEY CONCEPT

- All animals reproduce their kind.

KEY QUESTION 2

- Is the life cycle the same for every animal?

LEARNING EXPECTATIONS

- Changes over time
- Observe over time

Teaching Outline

- Read *Butterfly House.*
- Discuss the concepts of time, growth, and change as they relate to the life cycle of a butterfly.
- Have students trace the life cycle of a butterfly, communicating their understanding by referring to the text and illustrations in the book.
- Raise a butterfly from a caterpillar. Have children investigate the growth and development of a butterfly and keep an "Entomologist's Journal" of their observations and experiences.

(Note: Set the evaluation criteria for the journals with the children.)

Motivator

Read *Butterfly House* to the children. In *Butterfly House,* the author Eve Bunting explores the life cycle of a butterfly in the context of story. Concepts such as time, growth, and change are a natural outgrowth of this book. Children are extended the opportunity to observe and communicate their understanding.

Hands-on Activities

The learning and evaluation procedures in terms of expectations should be clearly understood before children begin.

1. Read *Butterfly House* again. Have children list the steps taken in the care of the butterfly from its earliest stages until the adult stage.
2. Raise a butterfly from a caterpillar. Invite the children to investigate the growth and development of a butterfly. Review the criteria for science journals. Have children keep an "Entomologist's Journal," daily recording their observations and experiences involving the development of the butterfly. Set criteria with the children for evaluating these journals before they begin them.
3. Make a list of the different parts of the butterfly's body. Use a stereo magnifier to look at these body parts. Children can record their observations then share them with a partner.
4. Take the children on a nature walk. Ask them to note all the animals they see, and have the children observe how these animals behave in their environment. Encourage children to keep a picture diary to record their observations over a set period of time.

5. Have children choose two animals and study their life cycles, comparing them for their similarities and differences. The children make a chart to record and share their findings.

Assessment

Book: *Butterfly House*	Rubric	Portfolio	Performance	Journal	Checklist	Observation	Conference	Peer/ Self
Life cycle					✔			
Observing growth				✔				
Insect identification						✔		
Picture diary				✔				
Comparison chart		✔						

Recommended Books for Animal Growth and Changes

How Do Flies Walk Upside Down? by Melvin and Gilda Berger provides a series of questions and answers about the characteristics, senses, eating habits, life cycles and behavior of different insects. A natural focus on inquiry.

Eve Bunting's *Butterfly House* traces the life cycle of a butterfly. This is a book that reinforces a sense of appreciation of nature and caring for all living things. The book also has a good focus on observing an insect's behavior using recyclable materials from the home.

The Magic School Bus Inside a Beehive, by Joanna Cole. This book encourages hands-on discovery, exploration, and investigation methods. The book is a factual account of a bee's life.

Where Are The Night Animals? by Mary Ann Fraser. Fraser uses lyrical text and realistic illustrations to help explain how nocturnal animals are adapted to living in the dark. This book helps the reader understand the world that comes alive under the cover of darkness — where are the night animals and where do they go during the day?

The Best Book of Bugs by Claire Llewellyn. In this excellent resource on life cycles, Llewellyn encourages children to think by providing clues to help them identify insects and their matching habitat.

Have You Seen Bugs? by Joanne Oppenheim. Using a verse format, this book encourages children to learn more about a wide variety of bugs.

Frogs and Toads, by Ellen Shultz. Children can learn about other kinds of animals in this book, which explores the life of frogs and toads.

Exploding Ants: Amazing Facts About How Animals Adapt by Joanne Settel. Children learn about animal habits that may seem disgusting for example frogs using their eyeballs to help swallow their food, are really wonderful adaptations that make it possible for a great variety of creatures to live and thrive on Earth as they find shelter, food, and safety in the natural world.

The Barn Owl by Sally Tagholm covers the span of one year in the life of a barn owl. This book provides information about the barn owl's physical characteristics and behavior patterns. Hunting, feeding, and nesting information is supplied in the story.

Bugs & Slugs by Judy Tatchell. This wonderful lift-the-flap book draws children into the pages through interactive techniques. Children are encouraged to lift a flap; when they do, they are immediately drawn into the world of bugs and slugs. Through questioning techniques students explore and discover new information about the topic.

Sample Activities

How Do Flies Walk Upside Down? by Melvin and Gilda Berger
Expectation: Characteristics of Animal Groups
In small groups use this question and answer book about flies. Have each group adopt a fly and observe its behavior. Have available hands-on tools such as hand lenses, bug boxes for the children to use in their investigation. Ask each group to think about and record one question they still have about flies. Have each group work cooperatively to research a possible answer to their question. Each group shares their findings with another group. They record their questions and answers in a cooperative big book titled: *Anything and Everything You Wanted to Know about Flies.*

Butterfly House by Eve Bunting
Expectation: Effects of humans on the environment
Many species of butterflies are now rare or extinct. Areas where they have lived have been destroyed, and their food source killed by pesticides. Collectors have also added to the problem. Have children make a butterfly house out of found materials. Following a study of the life cycle of a butterfly discuss reasons why it is important to return the butterfly to its own environment. As an extension to building a house, have children write newspaper articles on the danger of pesticides and how they can affect the butterfly's survival.

The Magic School Bus Inside a Beehive by Joanna Cole
Expectation: Observe life process of an animal
Read *The Magic School Bus Inside a Beehive.* Have children study the different roles bees exhibit in a day in the life of a bee. Divide children into cooperative groups. Have each group draw a bee's role (drone, worker bee, or queen) from a hat. Divide the classroom bulletin board into sections, and have each respective group complete their section illustrating the role of their group's bee.

Where Are The Night Animals? by Mary Ann Fraser
Expectation: Investigate how animals adapt to their environment
Read and discuss *Where Are The Night Animals?* Make available a wide display of books on night animals. Set up a rotating system whereby each child chooses a book about a night animal and takes it home to share with a parent/guardian. Encourage parents/guardians to read the book with the child and follow up with a night hike. (They can refer to the class newspaper for details on how and why to do the night hike.) If possible, the child and parent/guardian should use an audio tape recorder or video camera to record their experience. Each child shares his/her experience with the class.

The Best Book of Bugs by Claire Llewellyn
Expectation: Group/classify animals
Read *The Best Book of Bugs* with the large group. Take children on a nature hike to observe bugs. Provide a variety of magnifiers and a survey sheet to record their insect sightings. In small groups, have the children sort and classify the bugs according to the data collected. Have one person from each group use an overhead acetate to draw their groups classification system. Present their work using an overhead projector.

Have You Seen Bugs? by Joanne Oppenheim
Expectation: Changes over time
Following a discussion on how bugs change over time have children adopt a bug at home. Encourage the use of a hand lens and a throw away camera to observe and record changes that occur during a three week period. Ask children to keep a photo journal of the significant changes they observe. They place their photo journals in the school library for all students to appreciate and learn from this experience.

Frogs and Toads by Ellen Shultz
Expectation: Investigate how animals change
Nature can be brought indoors. Caring for living things gives children the opportunity to practice taking responsibility and to develop nurturing attitudes. Bring in tadpoles for children to study the life cycle of amphibians. Make available magnifiers for their use. Have children make a picture wheel demonstrating the various stages of amphibians. (A picture wheel is similar to the kind of birthday card that has a circle that is turned until the right number appears in the window.)

Exploding Ants: Amazing Facts About How Animals Adapt by Joanne Settel.
Expectation: Investigate how animals adapt to their environment
Have available a display of animal books. In small groups, ask children to find out how the animal adapts to their environment. Have each group decide how they will share the information with the larger group. They may choose to present their information or make a display.

The Barn Owl by Sally Tagholm
Expectation: Effects of seasons
Read *The Barn Owl*. Have several copies of *The Barn* Owl available so children can work in small groups and study the life of the barn owl in a particular season. Have students collect the data they will need to create

a seasonal mind map on *The Barn Owl.* Encourage children to use text and illustrations in their mind map to indicate the appropriate data and the selected environment. Invite a naturalist to come to the classroom to provide input on the authenticity of their data. Set up a time when the children can be an eyewitness at a naturalist site.

Bugs and Slugs by Judy Tatchell
Expectation: Characteristics of animal groups
Read Bugs *and Slugs.* Make available a variety of magnifiers. Take children on a nature walk to observe bugs. Have children select an insect and make notes on its physical characteristics. Make available microscopes and slides of bug parts for children to observe and compare with their own observations. Have children share their observations with a Science Buddy.

Additional Resources

The Giant Book of Snakes by Jim Pipe. Copper Beech

Wetlands Nature Search by Andrew Langley. Joshua Morris

Walk with a Wolf by Yvonne Winer. Charlesbridge

3-D Bees & Micro Fleas by Shar Levine. Sommerville House

Wings, Stings & Wrigley Things by Martin Jenkins. Candlewick Press

The Usborne Illustrated Encyclopedia — The Natural World by David Duthie. Usborne

Eyewitness Books – Insects by Lawrence Mound. Stoddart

Two Bad Ants by Chris Van Allsburg. Houghton Mifflin

Ladybug Ladybug, Where Are You? by Cyndy Szekeres. Golden

Looking At Insects by David Suzuki. Stoddart

Miss Spider's Tea Party by David Kirk. Scholastic

Insects – A Close-up Look by Peter Seymour. Macmillan

Who's Hiding Here? by Yoshi. Picture Book Studio

The Very Quiet Cricket by Eric Carle. Putnam

Owl Lake by Tejima. Philomel Books

Wolf Island by Celia Godkin. Fitzhenry & Whiteside

Crafty Chameleon by Mwenye Hadithi. Hodder/Stoughton

The Night Music by Violet Easton. Anderson Press

James and the Giant Peach by Roald Dahl. Puffin

The Tarantula in My Purse, by Jean Craighead George

Bugs for Lunch by Margery Facklam

The Ant Bully by John Nickle

Author/Title/Type	Basic Concepts	Science Process Skills	Equipment Used
How Do Flies Walk Upside Down? *Questions & Answers About Insects* *Berger, Melvin & Gilda* *(Inquiry, Information, Discovery & Exploration)*	Community Life Change Growth Interrelationships	Classifying Communicating Inferring Predicting	Binoculars
Butterfly House *Bunting, Eve* *(Storybook)*	Community Life Change Time Growth Interrelationships Technology	Observing Communicating Manipulating Materials & Equipment	Variety of construction materials e.g., jar, shoe box
The Magic School Bus Inside a Beehive *Cole, Joanna* *(Storybook, Discovery & Exploration)*	Community Life Change Growth Interrelationships	Observing Classifying Communicating Experimenting Making Models Manipulating Materials & Equipment	Magnifiers Microscopes Microscope Slides Binoculars
Where Are The Night Animals? *Fraser, Mary Ann* *(Storybook)*	Community Life Change Interrelationships	Observing Classifying Communicating Experimenting	Viewers
The Best Book of Bugs *Llewellyn, Claire* *(Information, Discovery & Exploration)*	Time Community Life Change Growth	Observing Classifying Communicating	Binoculars Magnifiers
Have You Seen Bugs? *Oppenheim, Joanne and Ron Broda* *(Poetry, Inquiry)*	Community Life Change Growth Interrelationships	Observing Classifying Communicating	Hand Lense
Frogs & Toads *Shultz, Ellen* *(Poetry, Inquiry)*	Community Life Change Growth Interrelationships	Observing Classifying Communicating	
Exploding Ants: Amazing Facts About How Animals Adapt *Settel, Joanne* *(Discovery & Exploration, Inquiry)*	Community Life Change Growth Interrelationships	Observing Classifying Communicating	Magnifiers
The Barn Owl *Tagholm, Sally* *(Storybook)*	Life Change Growth	Observing Communicating	Binoculars
Bugs & Slugs *Tatchell, Judy* *(Inquiry, Pop-Up, Discovery & Exploration)*	Time Life Change Growth	Observing Classifying Communicating Manipulating Materials & Equipment	

EARTH & SPACE SYSTEMS STRAND
Literature

```
                    ( EARTH & SPACE SYSTEMS STRAND
                              Literature )
```

CYCLES	AIR & WATER	SOILS	ROCKS & MINERALS	WEATHER	SOLAR SYSTEM
How Do You Know It's Fall? Allan Fowler	Water Frank Asch	Soil Karen Bryant-Mole	Nature & Science of Rocks Jane Burton	Can it rain Cats & Dogs? Questions & Answers About Weather Melvin & Gilda Berger	Inventions From Outer Space David Baker
How Do You Know It's Spring? Allan Fowler	Windy Days Caroline Bauer	Firefly Nature Encyclopedia David Burnie	The Magic School Bus Inside the Earth Joanna Cole	Dr. Fred's Weather Watch Fred Bortz	Do Stars Have Points? Melvin & Gilda Berger
How Do You Know It's Summer? Allan Fowler	Experiment with Weather Miranda Bower	Earthsearch John Cassidy	Archaeologists Dig For Clues Kate Duke	Flash, Crash, Rumble & Roll Franklyn Branley	The Magic School Bus Lost in the Solar System Joanna Cole
Sun Up, Sun Down Gail Gibbons	Feel the Wind Arthur Dorros	Marshes & Swamps Gail Gibbons	Earth Alive Sandra Markle	The Magic School Bus Inside a Hurricane Joanna Cole	Let's Look at the Planets Laura Driscoll
Spring Ron Hirschi	Science with Weather Rebecca Heddle Paul Shipton	Rocks & Soils Maria Gordon	Collecting Things Kate Needham	Nature's Fury The Power Station Andrew Gutelle	Space Station Science Marianne Dyson
What Makes It Rain? Susan Mayes	Drop In My Drink Meredith Hooper	How A Plant Grows Bobbie Kalman	The Best Book of Fossils, Rocks & Minerals Chris Pellant	First Guide Weather Jonathan Kahl	The Incredible Journey to the Edge of the Universe Nicholas Harris Joanne Turner
Why Do Seasons Change? Christopher Maynard	What Makes It Rain? Susan Mayes	Earth In Danger Steve Pollock	Milo and the Magical Stone Marcus Pfister	Weather at your Fingertips Judy Nayer	Space Hopping Nigel Hembest
Fall Maria Rius	Water's Way Lisa Peters	Erosion Joshua Rutten	First Field Guide Rocks & Minerals Edward Ricciuti Margaret Carruthers	Weather Chris Oxlade	The Starry Sky Patrick Moore
Autumn Gail Saunders-Smith	The Water's Journey Elonare Schmidt	Rocks & Soils Robert Snedden	Usborne Science & Experiments Our World Richard Spurgeon	Tornadoes Seymour Simon	Space at your Fingertips Judy Nayer
Why Is Night Dark? Sophia Tahta	Water: Simple Experiments for Young Scientists Larry White	Erosion Sherie Winer	Eyewitness Rocks & Minerals Dr. R.F. Symes	Weather Seymour Simon	One Small Square Donald Silver

Earth and Space Systems Strand

The Earth and Space Systems strand deals with the science and technology of our planet and space exploration. Children begin this strand by considering familiar events: the cycles of day/night and the changing seasons. As the children's knowledge and experiences are expanded, they move to topics, such as the solar system and stars. The Earth and Space Systems strand leads children naturally to using observation and scientific inquiry skills. They will explore the environment, the use and abuse of Earth's resources, and impact of technology on our knowledge, understanding, and ability to explore the Earth and the solar system.

Children are sensorial explorers; they take in knowledge best through hands-on, experiential learning opportunities. Teachers can help children become better observers by providing a variety of activities that require the children to use all five senses.

Investigations for Earth and Space Systems are of great interest to children because many of the topics are directly related to events and things the children have *likely* observed and wondered about. However, it is important to recognize that it is all too easy to let an exploration of Earth and Space Systems become static. I have observed this firsthand: My six-year-old grandson Ben and I were at a local science center, looking at a beautiful display of rocks and crystals. After a very brief time, Ben uttered, "Can we get to the *fun* stuff for kids? You know, the experiments you get to *do!*" It is critical in science, particularly for younger children, that teachers provide numerous hands-on activities for this exciting exploration stage of children's development.

The Earth and Space Systems strand focuses on six topics: Cycles; Air and Water; Soils; Rocks and Minerals; Weather; and the Solar System. Through studying the Earth and Space Systems strand, children are expected to develop skills of inquiry, design, and communication. They will develp an understanding of how wind, water, and ice, through the processes of erosion, transportation, and deposition, reshape the Earth's landscape. This provides a natural introduction to exploring how humans can prevent these changes and how they sometimes adapt to them. Children will also discover how various technologies are used in the world outside the school. Today, we are already reaping the benefits of space technology. Robotic technology that was used for exploring space is now being applied to human needs on Earth. SPAR's robotic Canadarm was used on space shuttle missions. The robotic technology was continued at numerous research facilities to investigate the possibility of using automated limbs for prosthetics. Today, robotic limbs are used for a number of tasks, including prosthetic thumbs and fingers. Scientists at NASA conducted years of research and have developed robotic hands that can carry out highly complex tasks for disabled people and for industry.

Space Research Benefits Humankind

Insulation developed to cope with extremes of heat and cold in space is now finding other uses on Earth. At even the lowest temperatures comfort and safety are yours with the development of the thermal glove.

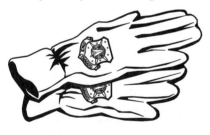

Space Technology and Your Feet

Athletic shoes that have an air pressure cushion at the midsole are based on space technology. The feature is an adaptation of the footwear in the spacesuits of astronauts. In running shoes, the adaptation offers more comfort and an even distribution of weight as the athlete runs.

Topic Summary

There are hundreds of different kinds of rocks, but each can be classified into one of three categories that describe the way different kinds of rock were formed: igneous, metamorphic, or sedimentary. Young children will often look at a rock and be more interested in assigning it a name themselves than in learning the geologist's classification system. Children often name rocks based on what they see. My grandson and I examined a rock known as Jasper. "Why is it called Jasper when it looks like a pizza?" Avery wanted to know. Sure enough, the specimen had patches of different shapes and colors covering its surface — like a pizza.

Many people become so fascinated by a particular kind of object or subject, they start a collection. Collections run the gamut from stamps to highly technical live steam model trains to rocks and fossils. Children are ardent collectors — as many parents can testify. The Earth and Space Systems provides several opportunities for children to become interested in beginning some sort of collection. Rock collecting is a popular choice. Children may sort their rocks by size, color, shape, and eventually broaden their interest and they begin sorting and identifying their specimens according to the geogological system. (And it seems that once a rock collector, always a rock collector!) There are other topics in the Earth and Space Systems strand that may encourage a student to start a collection. It is satisfying to see these children's enthusiasm grow. A child who was a reluctant young scientist before may suddenly develop not only a passion for one item, but for science and how the disciplines interconnect.

Topic Organizer

Rocks and Minerals provides an overview of ten science books that focus on the topic. See page 71.

Learning Expectations for the Topic

- Physical properties of rocks and minerals
- Classification of rocks and minerals
- Erosion of landscape
- Effects of humans on landscape
- Comparing different rocks from the environment
- Effect of wind, water and ice on landscape

KEY CONCEPT	LEARNING EXPECTATIONS
• There are many kinds of rocks.	• Physical properties of rocks and minerals
KEY QUESTION 1	• Comparing different rocks from the environment
• What is the surface of Earth's crust made of?	• Classification of rocks and minerals

Teaching Outline

- Step One Record what students know about rocks and minerals.
- Step Two List questions students have about rocks.
- Step Three Share the book, *Rocks and Minerals*, by Dr. R. F. Symes.
- Step Four Discuss the information put forth in the book.

- Step Five Develop a cooperative web incorporating the thoughts and ideas in the book.
- Step Six Plan activities to extend the students' learning.

Dr. Symes identifies the various types of rocks and minerals found on Earth. Colored illustrations and an easy-to-read text make the book very useful for young "rock hounds." Concepts covered in the book include:

- There are many kinds of rocks
- Rock imprints of ancient plants and animals are called fossils
- There are three categories of rocks

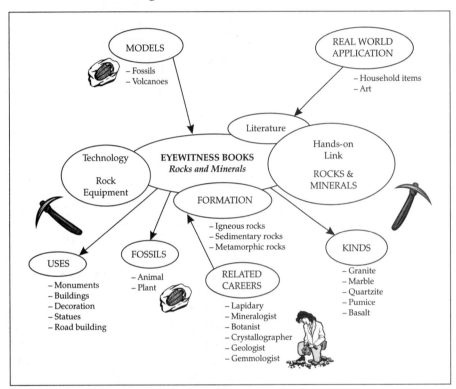

Motivator

Take children on a hunt for rocks and minerals. Have children take on the role of rock hound as they begin to collect rocks and minerals for their own personal collection. Inspire children to look for rocks and minerals in their natural state. Encourage children to take along the necessary equipment such as pen, pencil, masking tape and permanent markers (for labels), hand lens, container and, if accessible, a geological hammer. In my Grade 4/5 class, students elected to take along an old lunch pail to carry their rocks and minerals in as they found them. Following the rock hunt the students brought in a Styrofoam egg carton to display their rock collection. This worked extremely well. It's a good idea to take along a good guide book, for example, *First Field Guide Rocks And Minerals*, to identify any rocks or minerals they found. Have children label each rock and/or mineral with its name and the place where it was found.

Making, organizing and sharing collections of things of scientific interest is one of the very best ways to learn more about using scientific skills and processes. Children are constantly observing, exploring, investigating, experimenting, inferring, classifying, and evaluating throughout this experience. Look for, *Collecting Things* by Kate Needham. This is an excellent reference book to have in your classroom. Topics such as "What shall I collect?" "Where will I find things?" and "Storage and Display" are covered well. As a teacher of all grades, I have observed the excitement children exhibit when they are busy putting together their own personal collection and then sharing it with their classmates. In my role as administrator of an elementary school I encourage students of every grade level to bring to school their own personal collections. These collections are placed in the school display case for parents and students to ask questions, acquire new knowledge and learn more about the world around them.

Hands-on Activities

The learning and evaluation procedures in terms of expectations should be clearly understood before children begin.

1. Provide a collection of rocks and minerals for the students. Have children sort and classify them by size, weight, texture, and color. Ask students to make a chart showing the results of their investigation. Create a display of the rock and mineral specimens and post the children's charts alongside the display.
2. Ask students to research the three types of rocks introduced in Dr. Symes' book. Encourage the students to collect samples of these rocks and bring them to school. Provide magnifiers so they may observe them closely. Have students sort and classify the rocks according to type. Challenge students to find a way to present their results.
3. Read *The Magic School Bus Inside the Earth* to the students. Discuss the many ways rocks are used. Ask students to select five rocks from their personal collection, identify each rock's type, make a sketch of the rocks, and tell how and where they are used. Students share their collection and information with a friend.
4. Take children on a class walk in the school yard. Have each student select one specimen that interests them the most. Ask the children to do further research on the specimen and create a page with a sketch and textual information for a class field guide that is to be placed in the school library.
5. Set up a discovery center. Place geological hammers at the site. Have students break some of their rocks to make predictions about the kinds of rock categories their rock collection represents. Ask children to explain the reason for their choices.
6. Have students research ways to grow crystals. Ask students to select one of the methods and make their own crystal garden. Caution them to follow the directions carefully. To make a giant crystal, take out the biggest crystal with tweezers. Put it into a fresh container of the same solution, and it will keep on growing. Display all crystal results.

Assessment

Book: *Eyewitness Books — Rocks and Minerals*	Rubric	Portfolio	Performance	Journal	Checklist	Observation	Conference	Peer/ Self
Classification chart					✔			
Manipulating materials			✔					
Rock specimens								
Class book								
Rock discovery						✔		
Crystal investigation							✔	

Assessment Tip: Peer- and Self-Assessment

Self-assessment occurs when students evaluate their own work. Peer-assessment occurs when a student's work is evaluated by other students in the class.

KEY CONCEPTS
- **Old plants and animals left prints in rocks.**

KEY QUESTION 2
- **What can we find out from fossils?**

LEARNING EXPECTATIONS
- **Compare different rocks from the environment**
- **Effect of wind, water, and ice on landscape**

Teaching Outline

- Step One Record all the things students know about fossils.
- Step Two List questions students still have about fossils.
- Step Three Read *The Best Book of Fossils, Rocks, and Minerals.*
- Step Four Discuss the ideas put forth in the book.
- Step Five Develop a cooperative web incorporating the thoughts and ideas from the book.
- Step Six Plan activities to extend the students' learning.

Motivator

Read *The Best Book of Fossils, Rocks, and Minerals* to the children. This book investigates everything about Earth's fossils and rocks and minerals, from their formation to their uses and beauty. Throughout the story, Pellant provides great insight on how children can become expert fossil hunters. There are plenty of opportunities for teachers to plan hands-on activities from the storyline. For example, students may create a classification chart presenting the type of crystals or make their own timeline of the history of fossils. These activities will enhance science process skills such as observation, classification, communication, making models and manipulating equipment and materials.

Hands-on Activities

The learning and evaluation procedures in terms of expectations should be clearly understood before children begin.

1. Make accessible to the students a variety of fossils. Ask students to use a hand lens to observe them carefully. Have children record the appearance of the fossils in a log book, make their own drawings of each fossil and note the characteristics of the fossil and the rock in which it was embedded.

2. Shapes of animals and plants which lived millions of years ago are sometimes found in sedimentary rocks. These are fossils. Paleontologists go out into the field to collect fossils. Invite the students to do the following activity. Imagine you are a paleontologist and you are preparing to go on a fossil hunt. Collect everything you would take with you to go about finding fossils. Demonstrate how the equipment would be used. List five easy steps that tell a friend how a scientist goes about locating fossils.

3. Fossils found in rock provide a record of events that occurred around the time the rock was formed. For example, fossils show that the earliest birds had three fingered hands on the tips of their wings. (*Discover Mysteries of the Past & Present* by Katherine Grier). Without fossils we would have little or no record of living things which are now extinct. Have children use a computer software package on *Creating a Timeline,* indicating where, when, and what type of fossils were found in the school yard by individuals in the classroom.

4. Have students bring in examples of fossils they collected with their parent/guardian's help. Provide a variety of magnifiers for children to make their observations. Ask children to illustrate a page of one of their fossils for a big book, titled, *A Paleontologists' Guide.* Place the big book in the library for all children to use.

Assessment

Book: *The Best Book of Fossils, Rocks & Minerals*	Rubric	Portfolio	Performance	Journal	Checklist	Observation	Conference	Peer/ Self
Fossil observation				✔				
Fossil preparation					✔			
Fossil timeline			✔					
Paleontologist's guide				✔				

Recommended Books for Rocks and Minerals

Nature & Science of Rocks by Jane Burton is one of the "Exploring the Science of Nature Series" books. Colored photos and text explain science concepts in terms that children can understand. Features such as sidebars, activities and experiments, an additional reading section, and suggestions for complementary videos and websites make this book an asset for children's use in the classroom.

The Magic School Bus Inside the Earth by Joanna Cole provides an in-depth look at rocks and minerals. Associated vocabulary is introduced throughout the text, and facts about rocks and minerals are recorded and can be previewed at a glance. A complete picture of a student rock collection and a vocabulary chart at the end of the book provide a reference for teachers and students to reflect on their learning.

Archaeologists Dig For Clues by Kate Duke invites children on an archaeological dig. Children are encouraged to make some exciting discoveries about how scientists learn about the past. Duke provides opportunities for children to explore challenging concepts and includes hands-on activities that children can do themselves.

Earth Alive by Sandra Markle provides detailed information on the many ways in which the Earth is constantly changing. For example, changes caused by earthquakes and volcanoes. Children grow to understand that there are some places where we can see what an active, constantly changing world the Earth really is.

Collecting Things by Kate Needham. Fossils are some of the oldest things you can collect. Needham provides original ideas for every would-be collector. It is full of suggestions about what to do with the things you collect and how to show them off. The book also includes useful tips about caring for a collection, swapping and trading, setting up a collectors' club, and finding out more about individual specimens.

The Best Book of Fossils, Rocks and Minerals by Chris Pellant is the perfect book for the budding explorer. This book investigates everything about Earth's fossils, rocks, and minerals — from their formation and uses to their beauty and mystery. Detailed illustrations identify rocks and crystals. Step-by-step pictures show how fossils are formed over millions of years. Children can find out how to recognize rocks and become an expert fossil hunter.

Milo and the Magical Stones by Marcus Pfister. The story begins with, "On a small island in the middle of the sea, a mouse named Milo makes an extraordinary discovery — a magic, glowing stone hidden in a deep crevice." This special effects book grabs children's attention right from the start. How will this discovery change the lives of Milo and the other Mice? Will it bring delight or disaster? The children must decide — halfway through the story, the book splits into two sections, each offering a different ending. This book involves children in the decision-making process, showing them not only the effect today's environmental choices can have on the future of our planet, but also the consequences inherent in all decisions.

First Field Guide Rocks and Minerals by Edward Ricciuti and Margaret Carruthers provides full colored spreads to help beginning geologists observe and understand over one hundred and fifty types of rocks and minerals. This book is a must for all teachers to have in their field-study library within the classroom. Children can refer to it often, and it is small enough to carry with you on field trips.

Usborne Science & Experiments — Our World by Richard Spurgeon is an introduction to the world of science. Projects, experiments, and activities appear throughout the book. For example, children are given easy step-by-step directions for growing their own crystals. This book helps children to understand the theories by putting them into practice.

Eyewitness Rocks and Minerals by Dr. R. F. Symes is an information book that identifies the various types of rocks and minerals found on Earth. Colored illustrations and an easy-to-read text make the book a very useful text for young rock hounds.

Sample Activities

Nature & Science of Rocks by Jane Burton
Expectation: Physical properties
Set up a rock discovery center in the classroom. Have children work in pairs to describe the texture of five rocks. Place a rock in a bag and have one child feel the rock and try to find the matching type of rock from the display table. Have partners change roles. Repeat the process for the remaining rocks. Ask children to make a summary chart describing the textures they experienced to share with other students.

The Magic School Bus Inside the Earth by Joanna Cole
Expectation: Classification
Teach the appropriate use of a Venn diagram. Have children identify several categories for classifying their rocks. Ensure that children establish criteria for each grouping. Ask them to sort their rocks into the categories they have established, keeping the criteria in mind. Have each group input their data on an acetate sheet for the Venn diagram of their results. Provide an overhead projector so each group can share their results with the other members of the class.

Archaeologist Dig For Clues by Kate Duke
Expectations: Physical properties
Hide a number of items made of rocks and minerals around the classroom. Provide a list of clues to help children uncover the treasures. Ask students to play the role of Archaeologist and use the clues to find the treasures. Set up a discovery table for students to place the items made of rock and those made of minerals. For example, drill bits(item) and their connection to diamonds.(mineral) In this case the drill bits would be grouped with the minerals.

Earth Alive by Sandra Markle
Expectation: Effects of wind, water, and ice on landscape
Make available a wide variety of books on earthquakes, tornadoes, hurricanes, and so forth. (*The Magic School Bus Inside a Hurricane* by Joanna Cole is an excellent choice to make when studying hurricanes as a weather disaster.) Have children choose one of the weather disasters and select an experiment to demonstrate how, for example, tornadoes work. Children will need to collect the appropriate equipment to do the experiment. They may plan to do the experiment with a small group of children. Then have the children explain to the others how the weather phenomenon affects or is affected by landforms.

Collecting Things by Kate Needham
Expectation: Classification
Have children bring in a collection of common things they have already developed or make a new collection. Gather input from the children as to how to sort and classify the items. Complete a wall classification banner displaying the different connections. To extend their learning, you may want to raise the banner and host a *Collectors Trade Fair* where each child has the opportunity to set up a mini booth displaying their collection. Invite children from other classes, perhaps a science buddy too. Provide a box inviting all visitors to submit questions they have about the collections or a specific collection and feel free to make a trade with any of the collectors. Plan to address the questions at a later date.

The Best Book of Fossils, Rocks, and Minerals by Chris Pellant
Expectation: Compare different rocks from the environment
Most fossils are found in sedimentary rock. Have children locate sedimentary rocks and break them with a geological hammer to expose potential fossils. Ask children to examine the fossils using a variety of magnifiers. Make available other books on how to make your own fake fossils. *Discover — Mysteries of the Past and Present* by Katherine Grier is a good reference for this. Encourage children to make their own fossil cast using modeling clay or plaster of Paris.

Milo and the Magical Stones by Marcus Pfister
Expectation: Effects of humans on landscape
Read the story and discuss choices humans have in looking after our Earth. Create an awareness of the many ways in which living things and environmental conditions affect each other. Discuss the importance of taking only samples that are allowed, and of leaving the environment as undisturbed as possible when you conduct investigative work in the field. Have children work in groups to develop an experiment that would demonstrate how humans affect the landscape.

First Field Guide Rocks & Minerals by Edward Ricciuti and Margaret Carruthers
Expectation: Properties of rocks
Have children use magnifiers to help them sort and classify a large number of rocks into their own six categories. Ask children to record how many of each type they have so they can make a bar graph showing the

results of their investigation. Extend their learning by asking children to find other ways to communicate the results. Children may want to use a computer software package to present their data in another way.

Usborne Science & Experiments — Our World by Richard Spurgeon
Expectation: Erosion of landscape
Erosion occurs after fragments of rock or debris have been produced by weathering. Have children read books such as *Usborne Science & Experiments — Our World* by Richard Spurgeon. Organize the children into groups of four, and ask each group to design an experiment to show how to prevent soil erosion. Children may refer to the experiment in Spurgeon's book that shows how plants prevent soil erosion. Children may want to make a model or simply manipulate equipment and materials to complete the task. Have children communicate their understanding to the whole class in a way they feel most comfortable.

Eyewitness Rocks & Minerals by Dr. R. F. Symes
Expectation: Physical properties
We are surrounded by rocks and minerals in their natural forms and also by the many articles which are made of rocks or minerals. Invite children to list some of the things we make from rocks and minerals. Challenge them to find an example of an object that represents each natural form. Students should be prepared to present their findings.

Additional Resources
_____

Sleuthing Fossils by Alan Cvancara. John Wiley & Sons

Rock Collecting by Roma Gans. HarperCollins

The Earth by Steve Parker. Granada

Everybody Needs a Rock by Byrd Baylor. Macmillan

Digging to the Past by John Hackwell. Macmillan

Step Into Science — The Earth by Steve Parker, Granada

Talk About Sand by Angela Webb. Franklin Watts

How A Rock Came To Be In A Fence On A Road Near A Town by Hy Ruchlis. Walker & Co.

Discover Mysteries of the Past & Present by Katherine Grier

Rocks & Minerals by Jack Challoner. Lorenz Books

How to Dig a Hole to the Other Side of the World, by Faith McNulty. Harper & Rowe

Rocks & Minerals by Dixon Dougal. Ladybird Pub.

What Is A Mountain? by Chris Arvetis and Carole Palmer. Checkerboard Press.

Earth & Space Systems Strand			
– Rocks and Minerals –		TOPIC ORGANIZER	

Author/Title/Type	Basic Concepts	Science Process Skills	Equipment Used
Nature & Science of Rocks *Burton, Jane* *(discovery & exploration)*	Time Change Interrelationships Technology	Observing Communicating Experimenting Manipulating equipment & materials Making models	Variety of hands-on equipment & materials
The Magic School Bus Inside the Earth *Cole, Joanna* *(story)*	Interrelationships Technology	All	Hand lens Artifacts
Archaeologists Dig For Clues *Duke, Kate* *(discovery & exploration)*	Time Change Interrelationships Technology	Observing Communicating Inferring Predicting Interpreting Manipulating equipment & materials	Hand lens Archaeologist tools
Earth Alive *Markle, Sandra* *(information)*	Time Change Technology	Communicating	
Collecting Things *Needham, Kate* *(information)*	Technology	Observing Classifying Ordering Communicating Manipulating equipment & materials	Hands-on materials Artifacts
The Best Book of Fossils, Rocks & Minerals *Pellant, Chris* *(information)*	Time Change Technology	Observing Classifying Inferring Predicting Manipulating equipment & materials	Hands-on materials & equipment Hand lens Tools for measurement Archaeologist's tools Artifacts
Milo and the Magical Stones *Pfister, Marcus* *(story)*	Time Change Interrelationships	Observing Inferring Predicting Communicating	Stones
First Field Guide Rocks & Minerals *Ricciuti, Edward &* *Carruthers, Margaret* *(information)*	Technology	Communicating Interpreting	Artifacts
Usborne Science & Experiments — Our World *Spurgeon, Richard* *(discovery & exploration)*	Time Change Interrelationships Technology Conservation	Communicating Experimenting Manipulating equipment & materials	Hand lens Geologist's tools Artifacts
Eyewitness — Rocks & Minerals *Dr. R.F. Symes* *(information)*	Time Change Technology	Communicating Interpreting	Pocket magnifier Hand lens Archaeologist's tools Camera Tools for measurement Compass Artifacts

MATTER & MATERIALS STRAND
Literature

PROPERTIES OF OBJECTS & MATERIALS	LIQUIDS & SOLIDS	MAGNETIC CHARGED PARTICLES	MATERIALS THAT TRANSMIT, REFLECT & ABSORB	PHYSICAL & CHEMICAL CHANGE	AIR & FLIGHT
What's That Smell? Claire Bowes	**Why Can't You Unscramble An Egg** Vicki Cobb	**What Makes A Magnet?** Franklyn Branley	**Sound, Heat & Light Energy At Work** Melvin Berger	**The Magic School Bus Gets Baked in a Cake** Joanna Cole	**Wings** Mike Bantock
Experiment With Senses Monica Byles	**The Pottery Place** Gail Gibbons	**Magic Tricks Done With Magnets Magnetic Magic** Paul Doherty John Cassidy	**Eyewitness Science Light** David Burnie	**Walter the Baker** Eric Carle	**The Secrets of Animal Flight** NJC Bishop
Of Colour & Things Tana Hoban	**I Spy Treasure Hunt** Jean Marzollo	**Science With Magnets** Helen Edom	**The Magic School Bus in the Haunted Museum** Joanna Cole	**Everybody Bakes Bread** Norah Dooley	**No Problem** Eileen Browne
Science At Work-Shape Eric Laithwaite	**Science Experiences With Everyday Things** Howard Munson	**What Magnets Can Do** Allan Fowler	**Giant Book of Science** EXP	**It's A Gas** Margaret Griffin	**Cutaway Planes** Clive Clifford
Who Uses This? Margaret Miller	**Solids, Liquids & Gases** Louise Osborne Carol Gold	**Playing With Magnets** Gary Gibson	**Sound & Light** David Glover	**Physics Experiments For Children** Muriel Mandell	**Advanced Paper Aircraft Construction** Campbell Morris
Science With Everyday Things Howard Munson	**Liquid to Gas & Back** Jim Patten	**Magnet Book** Shar Levine	**Science In Action Light! Colour! Action!** Tom Johnston	**Chemistry** Chris Oxlade	**Eagles & Birds of Prey** Jemima Parry-Jones
Listening & Hearing Henry Pluckrose	**The Big Block of Chocolate** Janet Redhead	**Super Science Stuck on Magnets** Kate Mason	**Energy & Light** Peter Lafferty	**Elements, Compounds & Mixtures** J.M. Patten	**The Usborne Illustrated Encyclopedia Science & Technology** Max Parsonage Tom Petersen
Eating & Tasting Henry Pluckrose	**Solid, Liquid or Gas** Fay Robinson	**Straightforward Science Magnetism** Peter Riley	**Water & Light** Michinori Murata	**Straightforward Science Materials & Processes** Peter Riley	**Welcome to the World of Bats** Diane Swanson
How Do Your Senses Work? Judy Tatchell	**Visual Factfinder Science & Technology** Brian Williams	**Janice VanCleave's Magnets** Janice VanCleave	**Light** Steve Parker	**Kitchen Science Experiments** Park Roxbury	**Air, Wind & Flight** Mick Seller
My First Science Book A life size guide to simple elements Angela Wilkes	**What Is the World Made Of?** Kathleen Zoehfeld	**Magnetism** John Woodruff	**Fun With Science Light** Brenda Walpole	**The Lady Who Put Salt In Her Coffee** Amy Schwartz	**Science of Flight** Kim Taylor

Matter and Materials Strand

Everything around us, for example, air and water, trees, rocks, people, and animals are made up of different kinds of materials known as matter. The Matter and Materials strand integrates the study of matter with the use of material in technology.

Literature Science Breakthroughs uses a literature-based approach to teaching the Matter and Materials strand, linking children's literature with science concepts and skills. Many teachers have a strong language arts background, and the literature-based approach to science in this book uses their strength in language to good advantage. Ten science books of varying genres (such as story, novel, verse) are suggested for each topic of study. Organizers such as webs and charts are included in the book to save teachers time in planning and to help them plan more effectively to ensure the children are involved in doing science. These organizers provide an overview of the topics and the recommended books. The ultimate goal is to move all children towards achieving the learning expectations through the use of the books that lead to hands-on discovery, exploration, and investigation activities.

Each topic is introduced by a summary. The topic organizer that identifies the books is noted in the margin. The learning expectations for the entire topic are provided after the summary. Each topic is then broken down into a scaffolded sequence of Key Questions. Within each strand two Key Questions for each topic are developed. For example, in the Matter and Materials strand two Key Questions from Magnetic Charged Particles are explored leading to opportunities for further cooperative planning and development of the topic by teachers and children in the classroom. The Key Questions evolve from the specific Key Concepts to be developed within the topic and build on what the children have just learned, while narrowing their focus within a given topic. Every Key Question includes Learning Expectations, Key Concepts, Teaching Outline, Planning Web, Hands-on Activities, and Evaluation Strategies to help teachers identify how the children will meet the expectations for science concepts and skills through exploration. Teachers can use the reproducible: *Template for Organizing Books* to develop the remaining topics in the Matter and Materials strand for example, Properties of Objects and Materials.

The study of Matter and Materials helps children develop an understanding of the properties of substances, foundation skills necessary for future study. An integral component of the study of Matter and Materials is children designing and making useful objects affording them the opportunity to apply their knowledge of the properties of the materials they are using. These experiences help children grow to acquire knowledge of aesthetic and ergonomic principles in the area of technological design.

The Matter and Materials strand focuses on six topics: Properties of Objects and Materials; Liquids and Solids; Magnetic and Charged Particles; Materials that Transmit, Reflect and Absorb; Physical and Chemical Change; and Air and Flight. It is expected that through the study of

Farady Proves Magnets Can Make Electricity

Japanese researchers have already created a train called a magnetic levitation train. There are two strong magnetic fields: one on the train and one on the track. These fields repel each other, so the train floats above the track. Since the train floats above the tracks there is no friction between the train and tracks so the train can travel at very high speeds.

Electric Eel Zaps Fish

Some animals carry electrical charges as a form of defense or attack. The electric eel for example, has cells in its skin that allow a charge to build up. The eel uses this charge to zap a fish, stunning or killing it, so that it can eat at its leisure.

Matter and Materials children will understand the basic concepts of matter and will develop skills of inquiry, design, and communication. Children will also learn to relate science and technology to the world outside school. This is particularly important in the study of Matter and Materials since we often look to the properties of materials in nature to help us discover new horizons in the future. For example, observing the burr and noting how it sticks to clothing lead to the invention of "Velcro". Velcro has continued to make its mark in the many ways it has been used in the development of new products such as fasteners in running shoes and more. As well, further study of adhesives in a manufacturing setting lead to the development of a new product, Post-it Notes.

Topic Summary: Magnetic and Charged Particles

The magic of magnets continues to fascinate young and old. Age has no boundaries when it comes to being curious about our world. Imagine a little iron snake darting to and fro guided by a spinning top. What causes the snake to move? Is it magic? These little mysteries are bound within the study of Magnetic and Charged Particles. Children will study various aspects of matter and through their investigations, they will learn to observe, collect data, communicate with their peers, manipulate equipment, hypothesize, predict, and experiment. Throughout the topic children will learn:

- Ways in which different materials affect magnetic strength and electric charge
- Every magnet has two poles
- The strength of a magnet depends on the types and combinations of the various materials from which it is made
- To describe their observations of static electricity and the conditions that affect it

Through these experiences children will increase their knowledge about the properties of materials that make them useful for specific purposes.

Learning Expectations for the Topic

- Strength of magnets
- Use of static electricity
- Materials affected by magnets
- Investigation of static electricity
- Polarity of magnets
- Design/construct a system that uses magnetic force to move objects
- Strength of magnetic fields

Topic Organizer

Magnetic and Charged Particles provides an overview of ten science books that focus on the topic. See page 83.

KEY CONCEPT

- **Magnets pull some things, but not others.**

KEY QUESTION 1

- **What will magnets pull?**

LEARNING EXPECTATIONS

- **Classify, using their observations, materials that are magnetic and not magnetic, and identify materials that can be magnetized.**

Teaching Outline

Before You Start

The Tricky Sticky Problem shows children using a problem-solving approach — identifying a dilemma and making a series of attempts to remedy the situation.

Prior to using *The Tricky Sticky Problem* to introduce the concept that magnets pull some things but not others, find a simple method to teach children the problem-solving process. In the study of science, this process is known as the "scientific method." *No Problem* by Eileen Browne provides insight into the problem-solving process. Embodied in Browne's story are these key elements of problem solving: a thinking strategy; use of critical and creative thinking skills; a means of analyzing a situation; a means of applying past experience and knowledge to the problem; a focus on reaching a specific goal; a series of steps in any given model; and a recognition that steps are recursive. Teachers can use Browne's *No Problem* to introduce and discuss the steps in the problem-solving process with their students. The problem-solving process involves reaching a specific goal through following a series of sequential steps.

When children are provided with a consistent method for solving problems, they generally use the new concepts presented, study their solutions to the problems, and come to a greater understanding of the concepts.

Problem-solving Steps

- Identify the problem.
- Define the problem.
- Explore solutions.
- Act on strategies.
- Look back.

- Step One Teach a Problem-Solving Model.
- Step Two Provide magnets and materials for students to use to explore and discover the properties of magnets.
- Step Three Record all the things students discover about magnets.
- Step Four Read the first two pages of *The Tricky Sticky Problem (Identifies the problem)*, then have children *(Define the problem)*.
- Step Five Have children *(Explore solutions)*.
- Step Six Have children discuss how they would solve the problem. *(Act on strategies)*
- Step Seven Read the remainder of *The Tricky Sticky Problem*.
- Step Eight Discuss the strategies and solutions for solving the problem.
- Step Nine Plan activities to extend the children's learning.

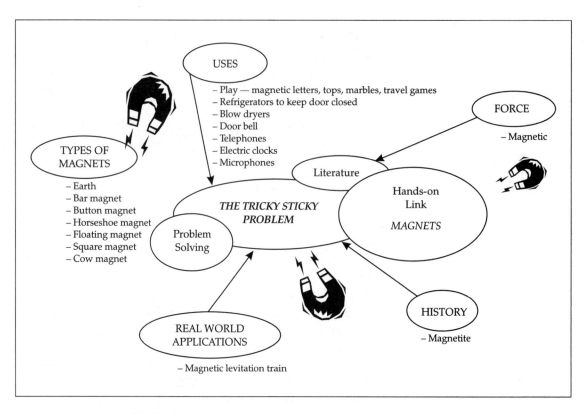

Motivator

Learning begins only after students are confronted with the problem. The best way for students to learn science is to experience challenging problems and the thoughts, habits of mind, and actions associated with solving them. Problem-based learning is a powerful vehicle for inquiry based learning in which students use an authentic problem as the context for an in-depth investigation of what they need and want to know. Problems embedded in stories such as *The Tricky Sticky Problem* can also serve as a springboard to providing problem-solving opportunities for children in the classroom.

The Tricky Sticky Problem begins with a group of children helping their teacher retrieve his keys from the drain. The children work cooperatively using different items to fetch the keys. Teachers can begin by reading aloud *The Tricky Sticky Problem*. Be sure to follow the suggested strategy for using the book found in the Teaching Outline. Reflecting upon their earlier exploration experiences with magnets, the children slowly uncover the properties of magnets.

Hands-on Activities
The learning and evaluation procedures in terms of expectations should be clearly understood before children begin.

1. Provide an assortment of magnets and iron/steel objects (for example, paper clips, ball-bearings) and non-iron/steel objects (for example, pencil, paper, aluminum foil). Have children explore freely how many of the objects the magnets will pull. Ask children to make a list

of other objects they find around the classroom that magnets will pull. Ask children to choose one of the items they find to share with the larger group.

2. Make books on magnetism easily accessible. Organize children into small groups. Ask children to design a game that incorporates the use of magnets. Allow time for children to play the game. Have children share one highlight of their creation in the large group.

3. Encourage children to become "magnet sleuths." Have children choose a magnet from a large variety of magnets. Ask children to move about the room touching things in the classroom to determine which things are attracted by magnets and which are not. Ask children to make a t-chart listing the results of their data. Children share their work with a friend.

4. Have children work in groups to outline a problem that can only be solved with the use of magnets. Ask each group to write down the problem and collect the appropriate materials others will need to solve the problem. Rotate groups through the problem centers.

5. Have children conduct a home survey showing the things around their house that use magnetism to function appropriately. Encourage children to get assistance from their parents. Have students create posters that show one of the most important uses of magnetism found in their home.

Assessment Tip — Rubrics

Rubrics outline and define levels of achievement and quality work.

Assessment

Book: *The Tricky Sticky Problem*	Rubric	Portfolio	Performance	Journal	Checklist	Observation	Conference	Self/ Peer
Magnetic objects			✔					
Magnet game								
T-chart					✔			
Problem solving	✔							
Poster		✔						

		Achievement Levels			
Curriculum Area	Activity Centre	Level One	Level Two	Level Three	Level Four
natural science	use natural and human-made objects to make color rubbings	attempts rubbings but does not persist until color is made	attempts all rubbings and observes which objects make color	completes all rubbings and compares which objects do not make color	completes all rubbings makes comparisons and draws conclusions

Motivator

Provide experiences for children that will uphold the motto: "fun in learning." Start at the children's interest point: Children love to go into toy stores. When a new toy is introduced, they are the first ones to explore and investigate the potential of its use. Although not a new toy, marbles have intrigued children for a long time. Just recently, my grandson, Ben, showed me a marble collection his dad put together as a child. We shared our excitement about the different kinds of marbles in the collection and the games that we could play using several marbles or just a few. Teachers can use marbles to encourage children to participate in an exploration of magnetic marbles. For example, make magnetic marbles available. Ask children to work in pairs with one child as the observer and the other, the investigator. The role of the investigator is to hold a marble in each hand and slowly bring his/her hands together. The observer records what happens. Reverse the roles and repeat the process. Each pair compares notes. Depending on the marble's orientation, they will see and feel the marbles either repel or attract one another. Have a student remove the plastic covering from a marble and find the magnet inside. Encourage children to design an experiment using the magnetic marbles, to develop a new game using magnets and/or to design a spinning top, demonstrating the role and function magnetism displays.

Hands-on Activities

The learning and evaluation procedures in terms of expectations should be clearly understood before children begin.

1. Children are excited about doing science to discover answers to their science challenges. Create a Science Carnival with six activity stations focusing on challenges that encourage children to explore the world of Magnetic and Charged Materials. Design each exploration as a discovery activity in which students use the scientific process. Provide children with the opportunity to demonstrate firsthand their understanding of the concepts associated with magnetism. Use *Usborne Science Activities — Science With Magnets* by Helen Edom, *Exploring*

Magnets by Ed Catherall, and *Straightforward Science Magnetism* by Peter Riley to help you plan appropriate challenges. The discovery activities you select for the students should closely relate to the appropriate Learning Expectations. Have children rotate through the six stations, completing the required hands-on activities and appropriate written communication. Students explain their learning and place their work in their portfolios for assessment.

Use the chart below, selecting assessment tools and techniques that are appropriate for your own six stations.

Assessment

Book: *Science Carnival*	Rubric	Portfolio	Performance	Journal	Checklist	Observation	Conference	Self/ Peer

Recommended Books for Magnetic and Charged Materials

What Makes A Magnet? by Franklyn Branley presents a model of inquiry and problem-solving as integral components of the scientific process.

Magic Tricks Done With Magnets Magnetic Magic by Paul Doherty and John Cassidy provides a collection of science/magic activities that explore the science of magnetism — and the tricky things you can do with magnets.

Science With Magnets by Helen Edom is packed with exciting scientific activities designed to help children explore the properties of magnetism. All the experiments and tricks are safe and easy to carry out, using ordinary household equipment and simple magnets. Real examples show how magnetism is used in hikers' compasses, door catches, and cranes, among other items.

What Magnets Can Do by Allan Fowler. This book provides excellent opportunities for children to use the science process skills, such as observing and inferring, as they explore and discover the true potential of magnets.

Playing With Magnets by Gary Gibson provides numerous science experiments. Activities are outlined with step-by-step procedures; results are explained: and further explorations are suggested. A "Fantastic Facts" section complements the text.

Magnet Book by Shar Levine. This book is full of experiments and accessible explanations featuring color photos and illustrations. A list of required equipment and safety tips is included.

Super Science Stuck on Magnets by Kate Mason challenges children to explore the mysteries of magnetism. This book includes four magnets and is packed full of exciting experiments and activities. Mason encourages children to make their own electro-magnet with materials included in the kit.

Straightforward Science Magnetism by Peter Riley introduces the basic science behind magnetism and presents experiments to show how it works.

Janice VanCleave's Magnets by Janice Vancleave presents a strong overview of the types and properties of magnets. It is an excellent resource with many opportunities for hands-on discovery, exploration, and investigation opportunities.

Magnetism by John Woodruff provides many ideas around Science Projects. Children are drawn to the ideas and are encouraged to become engaged in the whole process of doing a science project.

Sample Activities

What Makes A Magnet? by Franklyn Branley
Expectations: Materials affected by magnets
Read *What Makes A Magnet?*. Make available a collection of objects, such as nuts and bolts, a pencil, an eraser, and some paper clips. Ask children to work in groups using a magnet to separate the magnetic objects from the non-magnetic objects. Have a spokesperson from each group describe a typical magnetic material. Ask each group to create a page of text and illustrations that would contribute to all children's understanding of "what makes a magnet." Use a Big Book format to serve as a reference for all children.

Magic Tricks Done With Magnets Magnetic Magic by Paul Doherty and John Cassidy
Expectations: Polarity of Magnets
Have children work in pairs to observe and investigate what happens when the north poles of two bar magnets are placed next to each other; when the south poles of both magnets are placed next to each other; and when the south pole of one magnet is placed next to the north pole of the other magnet. Ask each group to create a rhythmic verse demonstrating their understanding of the rule about the behavior of magnets.

Science With Magnets by Helen Edom
Expectations: Strength of magnetic fields
Have available several copies of *Science With Magnets* and hands-on materials such as iron filings, horseshoe magnets, and bar magnets. In small groups, have children complete the experiments to find out more

about the forces associated with magnets. Have children pair up with another group to compare their findings. Ask each group to present their experiment and share their understanding.

What Magnets Can Do by Allan Fowler
Expectations: Strength of magnets
Set up a Magnetic Discovery World in the classroom. Have children in small groups use the magnets and materials to find a way to measure how much stronger one magnet is than the other. Ask each group to share one way they discovered to measure a magnet's strength.

Playing With Magnets by Gary Gibson
Expectations: Use of static electricity
Static charges produce sound. Read *Playing With Magnets*. Ask students to reflect upon their knowledge of magnetism. Ask them to relate their understanding of magnets to their hands-on experiences with static electricity. Invite them to show how static electricity is useful in the world outside of school in relation to sound devices.

Magnet Book by Shar Levine
Expectations: Investigation of static electricity
Ask children to bring in pieces of aluminum foil, a comb, and scissors. (Note: Children should *not* share their combs. One alternative is to bring in a brand-new package of combs.) Children are asked to cut the foil in small pieces and lay them on a table. Next they draw their comb through their hair and hold the comb above the foil pieces. Ask children to predict what will happen. Children should make their observations based on what they actually see. Ask them to explain why they got the results they did and to communicate their understanding to a friend. Provide a wide variety of books about static electricity so that children can check their answers about why they got the results they did.

Super Science Stuck on Magnets by Kate Mason
Expectations: Design/construct a system that uses magnetic force to move
Have children read experiment #9, "Can magnetism fly through the air?" Children collect the appropriate hands-on materials (paper clips, two square magnets, construction paper). Ask children to get in small groups and design an object that uses magnetic force to move.

Straightforward Science Magnetism by Peter Riley
Expectations: Strength of magnets
Provide a display of hands-on books about magnets, including *Straightforward Science Magnetism*. Have children design an experiment to demonstrate the strength of magnets. Ask children to make a presentation on their experiment.

Janice VanCleave's Magnets by Janice VanCleave
Expectations: Investigation of static electricity
Static electricity can build up when certain things rub against each other. Have children make a collection of plastic, wood, and metal objects. Ask children to sort the objects in two groups with Group One

containing all the objects that hold static electricity and Group Two, all the objects that don't hold static electricity. Children make a chart that identifies the materials that belong in each group.

Magnetism by John Woodruff
Expectations: All inclusive
Provide a selection of good children's books on the subject of "magnetism." Bring in a variety of materials, such as a large flat water container, wood, nails, and a strong magnet. Challenge children to make some magnetic boats using what they have learned about magnetism in their research.

Additional Resources

A Wrigley Book about The Magnet by Denis Wrigley. Lutterworth Press

Experimenting with Magnetism by Alan Ward. Chelsea House

Magnets by Julie Fitzpatrick. Hamish Hamilton

Learning Tree 123 Magnets by Susan Baker. Cherrytree Books

Electricity and Magnetism by Kay Davies and Wendy Oldfield. Raintree

The Science Book Of Magnets by Neil Ardley. Doubleday Canada Ltd.

Exploring Magnets by Ed Catherall. Wayland

Physics Experiments For Children by Muriel Mandell. Dover

	Matter & Materials Strand – *Magnetic & Charged Materials* –		TOPIC ORGANIZER	

Author/Title/Type	Basic Concepts	Science Process Skills	Equipment Used
What Makes A Magnet? *Branley, Franklyn* *(Inquiry)*	Matter Technology	Observing Experimenting Making models	Magnets Variety of appropriate hands-on materials
Magic Tricks Done With Magnets **Magnetic Magic** *Doherty, Paul & John Cassidy* *(Discovery & Exploration)*	Matter Technology	Observing Experimenting Communicating Manipulating materials & equipment	Round magnets
Science With Magnets *Edom, Helen* *(Discovery & Exploration)*	Matter Technology	Experimenting Communicating Manipulating materials & equipment Making models	Magnets – Floating, Horseshoe, Bar Iron Filings Compass
What Magnets Can Do *Fowler, Allan* *(Discovery & Exploration)*	Matter Technology	Observing Manipulating materials & equipment	Variety of magnets
Playing With Magnets *Gibson, Gary* *(Discovery & Exploration)*	Matter Technology	Experimenting Manipulating materials & equipment	Variety of magnets
Magnet Book *Levine, Shar* *(Discovery & Exploration)*	Matter Technology	Experimenting Manipulating materials & equipment	Variety of magnets
Super Science Stuck on Magnets *Mason, Kate* *(Discovery & Exploration)*	Matter Technology Conservation	Experimenting Manipulating materials & equipment Making models	2 Square magnets 2 Bar magnets wooden dowel copper wire steel rod plastic foam base
Straightforward Science **Magnetism** *Riley, Peter* *(Information)*	Matter Technology	Experimenting Manipulating materials & equipment	Variety of magnets
Janice VanCleave's Magnets *VanCleave, Janice* *(Discovery & Exploration)*	Matter Technology	Experimenting Manipulating materials & equipment	Variety of magnets
Magnetism *Woodruff, John* *(Inquiry)*	Matter Technology	Manipulating materials & equipment Making models	Variety of magnets

STRUCTURES & MECHANISMS STRAND
Literature

EVERYDAY STRUCTURES	MOVEMENT	BALANCE & STABILITY	PULLEYS & GEARS	FORCES	MOTION
How Tall, How Short, How Faraway? — David Adler	Inclined Plane — Patricia Arsentrout	This Is My House — Arthur Dorros	Force & Strength — Neil Ardley	The Visual Dictionary of Physics — Jack Challoner	No Problem — Eileen Browne
Building A House — Bryan Barton	The Treasure Hunter — William Boniface	Finding Out How Things Are Built — Helen Edom	The Visual Dictionary of Physics — Jack Challoner	Usborne Understanding Science Machines — Clive Clifford	Flash! Bang! Pop! — Janet Chahour
Finding Out About How Things Are Made — Felicity Brooks	Bicycle Book — Gail Gibbons	Up Goes The Skyscraper — Gail Gibbons	Lifting by Levers — Andrew Dunn	Bridges — Carol Johmann, Elizabeth Rieth	The Visual Dictionary of Physics — Jack Challoner
Our Big Home — Linda Glaser	Simple Machines — Deborah Hodge	Bridges — Etta Kaner	Pushing and Pulling — Gary Gibson	Science In Action The Forces Are With You — Tom Johnston	Kids Invention Book — Arlene Erlbach
And So They Build — Bert Kitchen	Bouncing and Rolling — Terry Jennings	Towers & Tunnels — Etta Kaner	Bicycle Book — Gail Gibbons	100 Experiments With Paper — Steven Mojie	Forces & Motion — Peter Lafferty
Samuel Todd's Book of Inventions — E.L. Konigsburg	Mighty Machines Truck — Claire Llewellyn	I Wonder Why Tunnels Are Round — Steve Parker	The Way Things Work — David Macaulay	Structures — Sally Morgan	The Way Things Work — David Macaulay
Oxford First Encyclopedia Science & Technology — Andrew Langley	On The Go — Ann Morris	Bridges — Ken Robbins	Physics Experiments For Children — Muriel Mandell	Science Activities With Simple Things — Howard Munson	100 Experiments With Paper — Steven Mojie
Mighty Machines Truck — Claire Llewellyn	Whizz, Click! — Diana Noonan	Squares — Catherine Sheldrick	The Carousel — Liz Rosenberg	The Usborne Illustrated Encyclopedia Science & Technology — Max Parsonage, Tom Petersen	The Usborne Illustrated Encyclopedia Science & Technology — Max Parsonage, Tom Petersen
animal house — Melissa Bay Mathis	Fun With Science — Brenda Walpole	Triangles — Catherine Sheldrick	Dr. De Soto — William Steig	Straightforward Science Forces & Movement — Peter Riley	Physics For Every Kid — Janice VanCleave
Animal Homes — Barbara Taylor	Clocks Building & Experimenting with Model Timepieces — Bernie Zubrowski	Bridges Are To Cross — Philemon Sturgess	Get It In Gear The Science of Movement — Barbara Taylor	Bridges Are To Cross — Philemon Sturgess	Wheels At Work — Bernie Zubrowski

Structures and Mechanisms Strand

STRUCTURE
• Any form that resists forces that would cause it to change shape and size.

MECHANISMS
• Used to create motion and consists of one or more simple machines (lever, inclined plane, wedge, screw, wheel-and-axle, or pulley) that perform a specific function.

Children instinctively begin to build with materials around them. The cushions (once companions of the sofa) and the car blankets soon disappear, and the children quickly redefine their use and function. Structures and forces are part of our everyday life from the simplest shelter of evergreen branches to today's multi-tiered towers. In the Structure and Mechanisms strand, children begin to understand something about structures and mechanisms as they observe and manipulate different structures in natural and human-made environments. When structures and mechanisms are combined, they make a system (for example, the brake system on a bicycle). It will be important in investigating the operation of systems that children first understand the parts of a system and how they function and then use this knowledge to understand the operation of the system as a whole.

Teachers may begin the study of structures and mechanisms by having children look at examples of structures and mechanisms in our environment. For example, on a recent trip to the Science Center, I had the opportunity to observe the inner workings of an escalator. With the transparent side facing me, I observed the pulleys and wheels at work. Complex machines, such as an escalator, use two or more simple machines to carry out a task. Complex machines include different combinations of the six simple machines — lever, screw, wedge, ramp (inclined plane), wheel-and-axle, and pulleys. Mechanical devices, such as an escalator, have parts that move. All machines that use mechanical parts are built to ensure that exactly the right amount of force produces the right amount of movement where it is needed. Forces hold the key to understanding structures. Throughout this strand children will be afforded many opportunities to design, build and test a variety of structures and mechanisms, and to use their observations to describe the kinds of forces and motion that affect their designs.

The Structures and Mechanisms strand focuses on six topics: Everyday Structures; Movement; Stability; Pulleys and Gears; Forces Acting on Structures; and Mechanisms and Motion. It is expected that through the study of Structures and Mechanisms, children will learn to relate science and technology to the world outside school. Teachers can motivate children by asking them to investigate easily understood technological applications such as sports equipment and how it functions. Take, for example, the structure and function of inline skates. The wheels on an inline skate rotate around axles to make the blade attached to the skate move in a straight line. Using real examples of structures and mechanisms children effectively make links to the real world. The children can also become involved in setting criteria, such as strength, safety, and reliability, to evaluate a product such as a piece of sports equipment.

Topic Summary

We are surrounded in our environment by a wide variety of human-made and natural objects and structures that have distinctive shapes,

Levers and Lobsters – A Simple Machine Connection

Many animals use their bodies to perform tasks with the help of in-built simple machines. A lobster's claws, or pincers, are third class levers. Simple machines such as the lever are used in a variety of different ways to make up more complex machines.

The Usborne Illustrated Encyclopedia Science and Technology
by Max Parsonage and
Tom Petersen

150 Story Building — An Environmental Solution

One answer to overcrowding is to build upward, constructing huge structures. Japan has proposed to build a Millennium Tower 150 stories high with a population of 50,000. It will carry 80 people at a time to sky centers and beyond where they can visit restaurants and shops, enjoy all forms of entertainment, travel to their apartments or places of work on other floors.

Eyewitness Books — Future
by Michael Tambini

Topic Organizer

Structures and Mechanisms provides an overview of ten science books that focus on the topic. See page 94.

patterns, colors, textures, and purposes. Just looking at the number of spider webs that exist or at the different kinds of building blocks one can manipulate is an overwhelming exercise. It isn't any wonder that we choose to simplify our lives and do what Scientists have always done — sort and classify. The different categories for structures; solid, frame and shell serve a distinctive purpose. It means we can sort, classify and compare both human-made and natural structures more easily using a valid, consistent and reliable framework from which to make our observations. This consistency, validity and reliability is what scientists expect when conducting a fair test. Very often this way of thinking becomes a significant factor in the development of new human-made products. We need only reflect upon picking up burrs on our clothes to make the connection between the properties of burrs and the invention of Velcro as a fastener. The use of fasteners goes hand-in-hand with structures . In exploring and investigating different types of fasteners and their uses, we can make more appropriate choices about things that have an impact on the strength and balance of a structure and the forces that act on it, and thereby improve the efficiency of its construction.

Learning Expectations for the Topic

- Shapes in structures
- Design/construct structures and explain functions
- Use of fasteners
- Action/response in simple systems

Teaching Outline

- Step One Record all the things children know about structures
- Step Two List questions children still have about structures
- Step Three Read *Building A House* and *Animal Homes*
- Step Four Discuss the ideas put forth in the books
- Step Five Develop a cooperative web incorporating the thoughts and ideas from the books
- Step Six Plan activities to extend children's learning

Motivator

Read a selection of books on different types of structures. Be sure to include support books such as *Zoe's Webs* by Thomas West and *Ants* by Trevor Terry and Margaret Linton, *animal house* by Melissa Mathis, *Finding Out About How Things Are Made* by Felicity Brooks, *Our Big Home* by Linda Glaser, and any other good books you can find on the topic. Each of these books provides great illustrations and text on how animals go about making their homes. In the large group, have children review the steps of building a house. Set up six centers with different exploratory materials children can use to build structures. At Center 1, students may be involved in building a structure using newspaper rolls. At Center 2, students might use the *Lego Dacta Intelligent House Brick Set* software to build a structure that is operated by a computer. Each center should provide a different experience for the children while they explore different materials such as toothpicks, straws, newspaper rolls, and boxes.

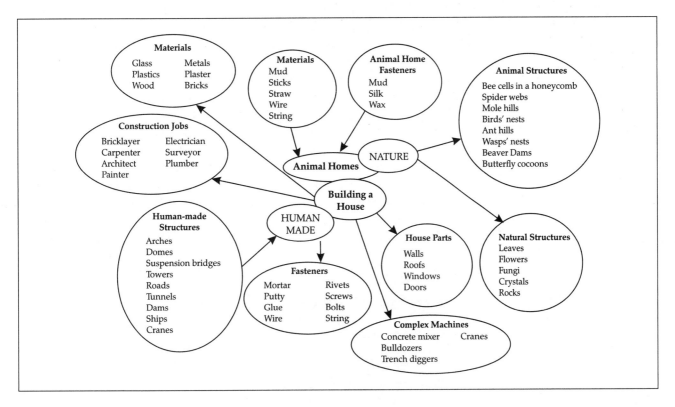

Hands-on Activities

The learning and evaluation procedures in terms of expectations should be clearly understood before children begin.

1. Have children use a variety of commercial building materials such as Tinkertoy, Meccano, Lasy, Duplo, Lego, Multilink, and Ramagon. Ask children to investigate the type of construction material and to identify how the type of material limits the style of construction.
2. A builder uses machines such as, cranes to help build homes. Ask children to use appropriate building materials to construct some working models of these machines.
3. Ask children to bring in construction tools from their home to make a class display. Have children find a partner and play an I Spy game with the tools. One partner chooses a tool. The other partner tries to guess which tool it is. When the partner guesses, he/she is required to share how the tool is used.
4. Make available to the children illustrations of the sequential steps involved in building a house. Have magnetic tape glued to each piece. Display a large framed steel surface. Have children manipulate the pieces and put them in their proper order.
5. Go on a nature hike. Choose one student to be a roving photographer. Have children look for structures in nature. When a sighting is made the photographer takes a snapshot of the sighting.

Assessment

Book: *Building A House*	Rubric	Portfolio	Performance	Journal	Checklist	Observation	Conference	Self/ Peer
Investigation						✔		
Models		✔						
I Spy Game								
Construction Stages					✔			
Photos		✔						

Assessment Tip: Portfolios

The Portfolio is an excellent means for demonstrating student growth over time. It should include a variety of assessments that offer evidence of process, product, and interaction. Provide children with prompts, for example, "This was a challenge because..." when reflecting on their own portfolio selections.

KEY CONCEPTS

- There are many different kinds of fasteners used in nature and in human-made structures.

KEY QUESTION 2

- What type of fasteners are used in nature and in human-made structures?

LEARNING EXPECTATIONS

- Use of fasteners

Teaching Outline

- Step One Record all the things students know about fasteners.
- Step Two List questions students still have about fasteners.
- Step Three Read *Samuel Todd's Book of Great Inventions*.
- Step Four Discuss the ideas put forth in the book.
- Step Five Develop a cooperative web incorporating the thoughts and ideas from the book.
- Step Six Plan activities to extend the students' learning.

Motivator

Place a variety of fasteners such as paper clips, zippers, nuts and bolts, glue, pipe cleaners, soaked peas, marshmallows, thread, and string in a box. Have children work in pairs. One partner turns away from the box and reaches in for an object. Without looking at the object the feel the object in order to identify it. The other partner records the guess, and then they switch positions. To complete the game, they open the box to see how many of their guesses were correct. In small groups the children are asked to discuss what job each performs in the world outside school.

Hands-on Activities

The learning and evaluation procedures in terms of expectations should be clearly understood before children begin.

1. Set up small centers with a wide variety of construction materials. Ask students to make the more common shapes (square, triangle, circle) out of construction materials such as, straws, pipe cleaners, and marshmallows to build their own structures. Challenge children to use fasteners and be ready to share the fastener and its function.
2. Collect a variety of fasteners used in building human structures and structures in nature. Ask children to establish criteria that describe the characteristics of the fasteners for both categories. Then have the children sort and classify the fasteners and prepare a classification chart. Extend the activity by encouraging children to talk about each fastener's use and function.
3. Ask students to think about a fastener that has never been invented. Have students work in groups to come up with a new invention for a fastener. Challenge students to make a model of their invention. Invite other classes to an Inventor's Fair, where students display their invention and show how it functions.
4. Ask children to investigate different kinds of glue for strength and ability to dry fast. They should use the following three types of glue: flour and water paste, wallpaper paste, and white glue. For a fair test, they must use the same kind of materials (paper) to test for bonding strength and ability to dry fast. Then they should try each glue with the different joints. Ask the children to write up the procedure in their Science Journal, and report their analysis of the results to the class. Encourage groups to discuss the similarities and differences between test results and the test procedures.

Assessment

Book: *Samuel Todd's Book of Great Inventions*	Rubric	Portfolio	Performance	Journal	Checklist	Observation	Conference	Self/ Peer
Fastener challenge			✔					
Investigation	✔							
Model		✔						
Investigation procedure				✔				

Recommended Books for Structures and Mechanisms

How Tall, How Short, How Faraway? by David Adler is a discovery and exploration book that provides opportunities for children to build science concepts through hands-on equipment and materials. Adler introduces and explains easy technological measuring tools. Practical explorations are provided for young students to achieve a deeper understanding of measurements and measuring.

Building A House by Bryan Barton provides an accurate and detailed explanation of the process, building materials, and support structure used in building a house. Barton helps children understand the stages in building a house from digging a hole to plumbing systems and painting. It is a great picture book for the very youngest aspiring builders.

Finding Out About How Things Are Made by Felicity Brooks. This book describes how masses of everyday objects come into being. Each stage of the manufacturing process is explained with the help of cartoon characters and illustrations. Children are afforded great opportunities to discover, explore, and investigate. Ask students to select an object and trace the complete set of steps in its manufacturing process, using a strip of adding machine tape to record each step.

Our Big Home by Linda Glaser. Glaser describes the many resources such as water, air, soil, and sun shared by living creatures on Earth. Young children usually think of their home as the structure in which they live; however, Glaser presents the Earth as a much larger structure of home.

And So They Build by Bert Kitchen addresses the design, construction, and function of structures in nature. This book provides a wonderful opportunity to speak about and develop positive attitudes concerning care of the environment and respect for living things.

Samuel Todd's Book of Inventions by E. L. Konigsburg. Belt loops, ladders, gloves — "Are these great inventions?" Ask Samuel Todd. Konigsburg lends insight into many inventions such as Velcro (which has uses beyond that of a fastener).

Oxford First Encyclopedia Science and Technology by Andrew Langley challenges children through a series of questions on how things are made. "Have you ever been to the top of a tall building? Have you wondered how they stay up?" This book offers exciting illustrations along with the text and contributes to children's understanding of structures and mechanisms.

Mighty Machines Truck by Claire Llewellyn. This book takes a close-up look at working machines. Photographs of real vehicles provide a wealth of structural and mechanical detail. Children are encouraged to compare machines and their work to everyday objects and activities.

animal house by Melissa Bay Mathis. This picture book begins with interviewing various animals about what makes a fun and cozy home. Each animal offers suggestions on the matter. The illustrations and text provide a snapshot of the animals' homes. Mathis challenges children to think when she says, "What if you built a house with all these things and more?" Children are encouraged to design their own inventive houses.

Animal Homes by Barbara Taylor leads children to explore and discover the structure of different animal homes. From termite towers to mud nests, to cozy cocoons and more, children can investigate animal homes above and below ground level. The book also includes information about animals that seek refuge in tide pools.

Sample Activities

How Tall, How Short, How Faraway? by David Adler
Expectations: Design/construct structures and explain functions
Share Adler's book along with *Workshop* by Andrew Clements. In *Workshop*, Clements shares the tools of a craftsman who makes carousels for fairs. Children learn that rulers are used for exactness, grinders wear away and more. Both books make a fascinating introduction to tools and their uses and to the role of technology in construction. Follow up with a Builder's Discovery Center where children can become familiar with building/construction tools such as screwdrivers and hammers. Have tools and materials (screwdrivers, screws, scrap wood) available so children can try their hand at using them in an informal way. Talk about safety and safe practices with the children.

Building A House by Bryan Barton
Expectations: Shapes in structure
Design/construct structures and explain functions
Read *Building A House*. Discuss with the children the various steps involved in the process of building a house. Have children work in small groups to draw the sequential stages. Extend their work by introducing children to the *Lego Dacta Intelligent House Brick Set*, which contains software and teacher support materials, including easy-to-follow building instructions. Have children use this set to build a simple house.

Finding Out About How Things Are Made by Felicity Brooks
Expectations: Design/construct structures and explain functions
Invite a builder to bring in a collection of building materials from the following categories: metals, plastics and wood to the classroom. Children work with a partner to categorize the materials, then the children share their work with the larger group. After the discovery process, the builder can discuss the structure of the materials and their functions.

Our Big Home by Linda Glaser
Expectations: Shapes in structure
Read *Our Big Home*. Combine this story with Barton's *Building A House* and *Animal Homes* by Barbara Taylor. Talk to the children about why their bedroom can be considered as a structure within a larger structure — their home. Ask the children to make a layout diagram of their bedroom, including any doors, windows, and furniture. Have the children bring in a shoe box. Provide a wide variety of building materials that the children can use to build their bedroom, using the shoe box as the structural shell.

And So They Build by Bert Kitchen
Expectations: Use of fasteners
Shapes in structure
Design/construct structures and explain functions
Read the book *And So They Build*. Provide a variety of materials children can use as fasteners, including natural and commercial materials. Natural materials could include chick peas, mud, and straw, while commercial materials might be marshmallows, pipe cleaners, and nuts and bolts. Challenge children to find a way to investigate the strength of the materials. Ask children to demonstrate their findings to the larger group.

Samuel Todd's Book of Inventions by E. L. Konigsburg
Expectations: Use of fasteners
Share *Samuel Todd's Book of Inventions*. Discuss what an inventor is and what skills an inventor needs to learn in order to make new discoveries. Compare an inventor to a scientist. Make a collection of materials that are used to keep things together, for example, zippers and Velcro. Have children examine these materials, and then try to invent a fastener of their own. Display all their inventions and discuss how their invention could contribute to the world outside of school.

Oxford First Encyclopedia Science and Technology by Andrew Langley
Expectations: Shapes in structure
Take children on a walk through the school neighborhood. Have children observe the different geometric shapes they can see in structures. Make available building materials such as straws and pipe cleaners for children to uses in creating their own structure. Have children share the shapes they used and tell why they chose those shapes.

Mighty Machines – Truck by Claire Llewellyn
Expectations: Action/response in simple systems
Use this book when the children have had a good variety of experiences with simple machines. Have a collection of model machines available for the students. Invite students to select one machine and investigate its functional characteristics. Have students explain how their understanding of simple machines has contributed to their understanding of an overall system, such as how a dump truck or a building crane functions.

animal house by Melissa Bay Mathis
Expectations: Shapes in structure
Design/construct structures and explain functions
Read *animal house*. Provide a variety of building materials. In small groups, have children plan and construct their dream homes. Children can keep an Architect's Journal, describing modifications they had to make to the design. Children present their models and identify the design and construction steps that worked as planned. They should select one example of the design and construction they had to modify. Display the models after the presentations.

Animal Homes by Barbara Taylor
Expectations: Use of fasteners
Shapes in structure
Design/construct structures and explain functions
Have children reflect upon the way in which different animals construct their homes. Ask children to design a home for animals, using materials found in nature. Ask them to create a fastener that would be useful in the animal's home. Have children tell why they feel their animal home will stand up to inclement weather and will provide the resident animals with protection from predators.

Additional Resources

Home Working: 101 Everyday Activities in Science and Technology by The Metropolitan Toronto School Board. Pembroke Publishers

Science Starters — Strong and Weak by Albert James. Macdonald Educational

From Blueprint to House by Franz Hogner. Carolrhoda Books

Bright Ideas Science by Jill Bennett and Roger Smith. Scholastic

Science In A Topic: Roads, Bridges and Tunnels by Doug Kincaid and Peter Coles. Hulton

I Can Be A Carpenter by Dee Lillegard. Children's Press

How Things Are Built by Helen Edom. Highgate

Messing Around With Drinking Straw Construction by Bernie Zubrowski. Little Brown and Co.

Building A House by Ken Robbins. Four Winds Press

Force and Strength by Neil Ardley. Franklin Watts

Science In Action — The Forces with You by Tom Johnston. Gareth Stevens Publishing

This Is My House by Arthur Dorros. Scholastic

Castle by David Macaulay. Houghton Mifflin

What It Feels Like to Be a Building by F. Wilson. The Preservation Press

Structures, The Young Scientist Investigates by T. Jennings. Oxford

<table>
<tr><td colspan="2">Structures & Mechanisms Strand
– Everyday Structures –</td><td></td><td>TOPIC ORGANIZER</td></tr>
</table>

Author/Title/Type	Basic Concepts	Science Process Skills	Equipment Used
How Tall, How Short, How Faraway? *Adler, David* (Discovery & Exploration)	Inquiry Technology	Manipulating Equipment & Materials Measuring	Building Tools Measuring instruments
Building A House *Barton, Bryan* (Storybook)	Matter Space Technology	Observing Measuring Communicating Making Models Manipulating equipment & materials	Surveyor's Tools Hammer Trowel Screwdriver Ladder
Finding Out About How Things Are Made *Brooks, Felicity* (Discovery & Exploration)	Matter Technology Conservation	Observing Measuring Communicating Manipulating equipment & materials	A large variety of equipment & materials
Our Big Home *Glaser, Linda* (Poetry)	Interrelationships Community Conservation	Observing Communicating	
And So They Build *Kitchen, Bert* (Information)	Life Change Growth Interrelationships Space	Observing Communicating	
Samuel Todd's Book of Inventions *Konigsburg, E.L.* (Information)	Interrelationships Technology Change	Communicating	
Oxford First Encyclopedia Science & Technology *Langley, Andrew* (Discovery & Exploration)	Technology Space	Experimenting Manipulating materials & equipment	Balance scale Video camera Variety of materials & equipment
Mighty Machines Truck *Llewellyn, Claire* (Information)	Technology	Observing Communicating Classifying	
animal house *Mathis, Melissa Bay* (Storybook)	Space Change Inquiry Technology	Observing Communicating Manipulating equipment & materials Making models	Blueprint Hammer Screwdriver Tool box
Animal Homes *Taylor, Barbara* (Information)	Community Change Space	Observing Classifying Communicating	

ENERGY & CONTROL STRAND
Literature

ENERGY IN OUR LIVES	WIND & WATER	FORCES	LIGHT & SOUND	CONSERVATION OF ENERGY	ELECTRICITY
Trains Gail Gibbons	**Experiments With Water** Ray Brockel	**The Science Book of Gravity** Neil Ardley	**Sound, Heat & Light Energy At Work** Melvin Berger	**Conserving The Atmosphere** John Baines	**Electricity & Magnetism** Peter Adamczyk Paul-Francis Law
Finding Out About Energy Terry Jennings	**Kites - Magic Wishes That Fly Up To The Sky** T. Demi	**The Inclined Plane** Patricia Armentrout	**Eyewitness Science Light** David Burnie	**Nuclear Power** Ian Graham	**The Science Book Of Electricity** Neil Ardley
What Is Balance? Viking Kestrel	**Science With Air** Helen Edom Moira Butterfield	**Pushing & Pulling** Gary Gibson	**Sound & Light** David Glover	**Geothermal & Bio Energy** Ian Graham	**Electric Gadgets & Gizmos** Allan Bartholomew
Where Does Electricity Come From? Susan Mayes	**Science With Water** Helen Edom	**Understanding Science Machines** Clive Clifford	**Flicker Flash** Joan Graham	**Water Power** Ian Graham	**Electricity** Karen Bryant-Mole
Energy At Work Marshall Jones	**I Wonder Why the Wind Blows & Other Questions About Our Planet** Anita Ganeri	**Eyewitness Science Force & Motion** Peter Lafferty	**Sound Science** Etta Kaner	**Garbage & Recycling** Rosie Harlan	**The Magic School Bus & the Electric Field** Joanna Cole
Archibald & the Crunch Machine Jenny Nelson	**Water Power** Ian Graham	**Motion & Speed** John Marshall	**The Boy With Two Shadows** Margaret Mahy	**Energy** Nigel Hawker	**The Usborne Young Scientist** Philip Chapman
Wind Ups Chris Ollenshaw & Pat Triggs	**Simple Space & Flight Experiments with Everyday Materials** Louis Loeschnig	**Experiment With Movement** Bryan Murphy	**Experiment With Light** Bryan Murphy	**Our Energy Supply** John Marshall	**Electricity** Simon De Pinna
Using Energy Julian Rowe	**Experiment With Air** Bryan Murphy	**Get It In Gear The Science of Movement** Barbara Taylor	**Mole Music** David McPhail	**Using Energy** Sally Morgan	**Energy & Power** Richard Spurgeon Mike Flood
The Merry Go Round Dog Elisa Schneider	**Experiment With Water** Bryan Murphy	**Janice VanCleave's Gravity** Janice VanCleave	**Sound Noise & Music** Mick Seller	**Keeping Water Clean** Ewan McLeish	**Janice VanCleave's Electricity** Janice VanCleave
First Technology Toys John Williams	**The Jumbo Book of Science** The Ontario Science Centre	**Gravity Simple Experiments For Young Scientists** Larry White	**Optical Tricks** Walter Wicks	**We Need Energy** Colin Walker	**Experiment With Magnetism & Electricity** Margaret Whalley

Energy and Control Strand

Most children are curious about flying objects. I was reminded of this recently, when I was at a restaurant with my grandchildren. They wanted something to do while they waited for their food. Both my memory and my skills were tested as I showed the kids how to fold paper airplanes. Soon airplanes of every shape and size were zooming around the restaurant, and it wasn't long before the employees joined in the fun, too! Then came the children's questions. "What makes airplanes fly — is it the wind? Why don't the wings flap? How does the plane stay up?" Even as I answered their questions, I was thinking of ways to use this experience in the Energy and Control strand.

Tornadoes and Bats – Linking Technology

All waves carry energy. Bats emit high squeaks that work like echo radar. The sound bounces off prey, enabling the bats to track it down. Radar waves can spot a tornado 20 minutes before its funnel hits the ground.

The Usborne Illustrated Encyclopedia Science & Technology

The Energy and Control strand introduces children to common forms of energy, energy conversions, and the uses of energy. In this strand, children will explore questions such as "Where can we find energy? How is it used? How do we know energy is involved?" When young children are asked to show their energy, they respond by jumping, running, pushing, pulling, and any number of ways they can imagine moving! (Interestingly, children demonstrate something about our overall understanding of energy: We define energy by what it *does*. Beyond that, we really can't say exactly what energy *is*. For this reason it is unfair to ask children "What is energy?")

Most children are curious about flying objects, whether the objects are animals with wings, leaves that drift to the ground in autumn, kites pulled high by the wind, or paper airplanes propelled by energy from our own muscles. Ask the children how we can use energy from the wind for fun and play. Expect answers such as sailboarding, sailing a boat, and flying kites. If possible, provide a concrete experience with wind, such as flying a kite. Through concrete experiences such as experimenting with devices that control the amount of energy used, children build their skills and fundamental understanding of energy that will lead them to a more complex consideration of the topic.

The Energy and Control strand focuses on six topics: Energy in Our Lives; Wind and Water; Forces, Light and Sound; Conservation of Energy; and Electricity. Throughout the study of Energy and Control, children will explore energy and its connection to the world outside the school. Energy conservation is an important topic that everyone can relate to. Scientists today are continuing to investigate new ways to access renewable energy sources. Children may not realize that energy from the wind is converted to electricity at "windmill farms" or that moving water is also an important source for generating electricity. However, someone has probably told them, "Please turn out the lights if you aren't using them!" More than ever, we need to help children understand that they can control the amount of energy they and their families use. The little things we do — turning off a light or putting in energy-efficient light bulbs — add up to a wise use of electricity. The more we all know about energy consumption and energy conservation, the more able we are to work together to become better stewards of our environment.

Topic Summary

Air and water are two of Earth's two most valuable resources. How can we use them as energy resources? Are they renewable? These are among the questions children will explore through hands-on experiments to gain an understanding of water and wind as sources of energy. Finding answers to other questions, such as "Where does wind come from? What can we do with it? How can we use it for energy? What can we do with moving water?" will allow children to discover that it is the *movement* of air and water that produces energy, and that air and water are not by themselves sources of energy.

Energy from wind and water make things move. Wind is moving air. The rotating blades of electric fans and blowing with your mouth also move currents of air. Wind flies kites, sails boats and turns windmills. The movement of running water and the rushing wind is converted into electricity by machines such as windmills and waterwheels. Energy from moving water can carry floating logs down a waterway. Creating opportunities in the classroom for children to demonstrate there is energy in wind and in moving water is critical in this topic. We must challenge children to find examples of how we can use wind energy and the energy from moving water. By designing their own wind- and water-propelled devices, children will learn about factors that affect the motion and control of such devices. We need to help children recognize that using wind energy is wise because wind is a renewable source of energy. And finally, we need to teach children to use electrical energy from moving water wisely. When children recognize the importance of protecting natural resources, conservation of our resources becomes a meaningful and purposeful issue.

Learning Expectations for the Topic

- Forms of energy
- Renewable sources of energy
- Moving water and air as sources of energy
- Design/construct a wind or water-powered device

<table>
<tr><td>

KEY CONCEPT

- There is energy from wind.

KEY QUESTION 1

- How can we use energy from wind?

</td><td>

LEARNING EXPECTATIONS

- Forms of energy
- Renewable sources of energy
- Moving air as a source of energy
- Design/construct a wind-powered device

</td></tr>
</table>

Teaching Outline

- Step One Record what students know about energy.
- Step Two List questions students have about energy.
- Step Three Share the book, *Science With Air* by Helen Edom.
- Step Four Discuss the information put forth in the book.
- Step Five Develop a cooperative web incorporating the thoughts and ideas of the book, and include the students' thoughts.
- Step Six Plan activities to extend the students' learning

Topic Organizer

Wind and Water provides an overview of ten science books that focus on the topics. See page 106.

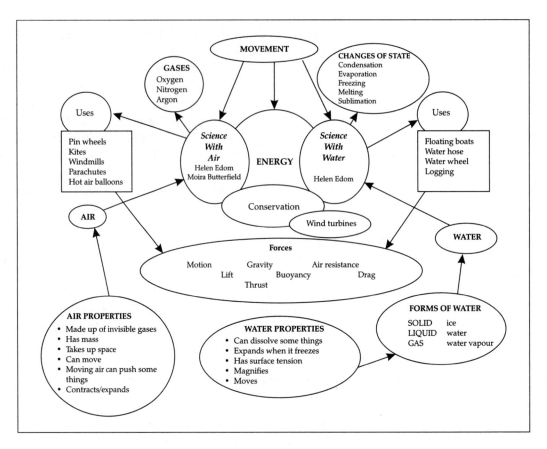

Motivator

Read the poem "Who Has Seen the Wind?" in *Windy Day — Stories and Poems* by Lilian Moore (or another short poem that that fits the topic). Take children outside to the school yard to explore and experience the signs of a windy day. Can they see clouds moving or a flag blowing in the wind? Are branches and leaves on trees bending and rustling? Ask children to make a list of the signs they notice and share it with a friend. This short exploration prepares children for the first hands-on activity noted below.

Hands-on Activities
The learning and evaluation procedures in terms of expectations should be clearly understood before children begin.

1. Share *Science With Air* by Helen Edom and Moira Butterfield. This book of experiments can help you emphasize how a scientist conducts investigations to solve problems and learn more about a topic.

   Using *Science With Air* select five activities and set up an exploratory and investigative center for each, including the hands-on equipment and materials. Explain the organization of the five activity centers and the specific task to do at each one.

   Provide a copy of Edom and Butterfield's book at each center. Encourage students to make notes about their observations and results by providing a "Meteorologist's Science Journal" where students can write up the procedure they used to do the experiment. Later, students can read these special journals and share their results with the larger group.

2. Ask children to think about the question, "Does wind have energy?" Use class brainstorming for their ideas and record them on a wall chart. Tell children that in the next activity, they will be required to do a peer assessment. Talk about what a peer assessment is, and with the children, develop the criteria for it. Organize children into groups of four. Ask children to think of a test or experiment to show that wind has energy. Video tape a demonstration of each group's test or experiment. When all the video taped demonstrations have been reviewed, ask children to complete a peer assessment of each group's efforts.

3. Have children discuss and list the ways they could use wind energy outside of school. (Common answers might include sailing boats, sailboarding, flying a kite, generating electricity, carrying a weather balloon, and so on.) Ask children to work with a partner to design and draw an object they could create which would show wind energy at work. Have children collect the materials and construct a working model based on their design. Allow time for a Wind Energy Exhibition where students can try out each others' creations.

4. Invite parents/guardians to the school to learn more about this activity. Explain that as part of the home/school learning partnership, children are to work with a parent/guardian to explore wind energy in their neighborhood. As part of the activity, the pairs are to take photographs of the wind energy examples they find. To assist parents/guardians in understanding the topic, invite a meteorologist to speak to the group about wind energy. You might also want to invite a photographer to talk about tips for taking photographs that will help others understand the subject. Finally, each child–parent/guardian pair is to put together a "photo shoot" of their learning. Host a Neighborhood Wind Energy Evening for sharing the photo shoots. Invite the meteorologist and photographer to join you again. They may be interested in seeing the results, and parents/guardians and children may have further questions for these experts.

5. Ask students to explore the properties of air and make a mindscape on air, including words and pictures that show how their ideas are connected. Assemble the mindscapes in a mural-like fashion for display in the school hallway. An audio tape prepared by the students to explain the mural of mindscapes makes the display an interactive way for children to tell others about their learning. In addition, you might include a box where other students can submit questions they still have about air. Address these questions as a follow up to this activity.

Assessment

Book: *Science With Air*	Rubric	Portfolio	Performance	Journal	Checklist	Observation	Conference	Self/Peer
Investigation	✔							
Video tape								
Model			✔					
Photo shoot				✔				
Mindscape & Audio tape	✔							

Assessment Tip: Performance-based Assessment

Performance-based Assessment allows for evaluation of both process and product. It can be used as a summative tool for purposes of evaluating the degree to which students have achieved the learning expectations.

KEY CONCEPT

• **There is energy from moving water.**

KEY QUESTION 2

• **How can we use energy from moving water?**

LEARNING EXPECTATIONS

• **Forms of energy**
• **Renewable sources of energy**
• **Moving water as a source of energy**
• **Design/construct a water-powered device**

Teaching Outline

• Step One Record what students know about energy from moving water.
• Step Two Share the book, *Science With Water*, by Helen Edom.
• Step Three Discuss the information put forth in the book.
• Step Four Develop a cooperative web incorporating the thoughts and ideas of the book and any new thoughts.
• Step Five Plan activities to extend the students' learning.

Motivator

Give each student a glass of water. Working with a partner, students are asked to identify what is in the glass, its uses, and its environmental connection(s).

Select five good science books that focus on water and its many properties. Excellent books include, *Mr. Archimedes Bath* by Pamela Allen, *Lester and Clyde* by James Reece, *The Water's Journey* by Eleonore Schmidt, *The Magic Bubble Trip* by Ingrid Schubert, and *King Bidgood's in the Bathtub* by Audrey Wood. Set up a station for each book. In groups of five, students read the book at their station and prepare a mini-play that demonstrates what they learned about water from the book. Allow students time to act out their plays and share their book with the larger group. Record their learning on a large Water Learnings Wall Chart for the rest of the students in the school to see.

Hands-on Activities

The learning and evaluation procedures in terms of expectations should be clearly understood before children begin.

1. Select five investigations from *Science With Water* by Helen Edom and set up five exploratory and investigative centers. Provide the hands-on equipment and materials for each investigation. Have students rotate through the centers, so they do all five investigations. At each center, provide an activity-specific Science Journal where students can record the things that worked and didn't work on completion of each investigation. Have students gather in a large circle to share the comments in the journals.
2. Ask children to work with a parent/guardian to create an experiment demonstrating one of the properties of water. Host an evening at the school where guests are invited to rotate through the centers and do the experiments to learn more about water.
3. Make available a large collection of pictures/posters showing how we can use energy from moving water. Place one picture/poster at each of the five stations. Have children work in cooperative groups to discuss the way energy is used in the illustration at each center. Ask students to do a survey around their house for one week of the many ways their family uses energy from moving water. Collect the data from each student and write it on the board. With the class, make a bar graph of the ways and number of times that energy from moving water was used in their homes. Post the graph in the classroom.
4. Make available books that show how to make a water-powered device such as, *Usborne Science Experiments — Energy and Power* by Richard Spurgeon and Mike Flood. Ask students to design and construct a water-powered device of their own. Host a *Techno Water Day* where students demonstrate their models. Ask students to identify how they might improve on their model.
5. Ask students to bring in their own materials for this activity, in which they build a waterwheel. Organize students into groups of five. Ask them to construct a waterwheel using *Usborne Science and Experiments — Energy and Power* by Richard Spurgeon and Mike Flood as their guide. (Advise them that they can modify the design found in the book.) They should identify and record any modifications they make to the design found in the book. Have students share their device, procedure, and any modifications orally with the larger group.

Assessment

Book: *Science With Water*	Rubric	Portfolio	Performance	Journal	Checklist	Observation	Conference	Self/Peer
Investigation	✔							
Experiment					✔			
Bar graph					✔			
Construct device	✔							
Model			✔					

Recommended Books For Wind and Water

Experiments With Water by Ray Brockel. Easy-to-do experiments with lots of opportunities for hands-on explorations and investigations.

Kites — Magic Wishes That Fly Up to the Sky by T. Demi. Demi weaves the tale of kites and the ancient Chinese tradition of decorating kites with symbols and images of animals that represent the kind of luck the kite-maker wished to attract. This book depicts many animal images and their traditional meanings. Instructions for making a kite are included.

Science With Air by Helen Edom and Moira Butterfield provides a collection of experiments and tricks to help children explore the properties of air using household equipment.

Science With Water by Helen Edom. This book contains scientific activities designed to help young children explore the properties of water.

I Wonder Why the Wind Blows & Other Questions About Our Planet by Anita Ganeri. This book answers childrens' most common questions about wind and other natural phenomena.

Water Power by Ian Graham. Many of our planet's major sources of energy, such as coal, oil, and natural gas, may run out in the first half of the next century. This book investigates some possible new sources, which must be identified and developed quickly and safely.

Simple Space & Flight Experiments by Louis Loeschnig. This book teaches children to use everyday objects like cardboard, thumbtacks, scissors, and a ruler to do simple, fun experiments that show the science behind aviation. Children learn how to make everything from Twirly-Whirlies to Kite Tales.

The Magic School Bus Ups and Downs by Jane Mason. A great book for encouraging hands-on participation. Lots of experiments on sinking and floating.

Experiment With Air by Bryan Murphy. Lots of opportunities are provided for children to explore and investigate moving air as a source of energy. Great hands-on activities.

Experiment With Water by Bryan Murphy. Children are provided many ways to explore and investigate movement and water as a source of energy. The book includes several hands-on activities.

The Jumbo Book of Science by The Ontario Science Centre. A wonderful collection of intriguing hands-on experiments. Topics range from how nature makes wind and soil to how magnifiers magnify.

Sample Activities

Kites — Magic Wishes That Fly Up to the Sky by T. Demi
Expectations: Design/construct a wind-powered device
Have students experiment with making kites. Invite a kite maker into the classroom to provide tips about things such as the best materials to use, the finished size, finished shape, and the best wind conditions. Ask students to design and construct their own kite. They should keep a record of the steps and stages of the process in a Kite Maker's Journal. Plan a specific day and time to fly the kites (weather permitting).

The Jumbo Book of Science by the Ontario Science Centre
Expectations: Design/construct a wind-powered device
Using tape, tissues, and pencils — children construct a simple device that moves in air. Children become "draft detectives" by using the device to find air leaks around windows and doors. The rest of the book is filled with other easy-to-do experiments and loads of interest-catching science.

I Wonder Why the Wind Blows & Other Questions About Our Planet by Anita Ganeri
Expectations: Moving air as a source of energy
Take children on a walk through the neighborhood on two different days. Record the weather conditions for each day. Ask students to observe and describe how things are moving (for example, quickly/slowly, up/down). Ask the children to list or draw all the things they see that indicate air is moving. Have them compare their observations from both days. Invite them to try to determine why there are similarities and/or differences in their observations for the two days. Create a big book of WHY questions using each student's data.

Water Power by Ian Graham
Expectations: Renewable sources of energy
Water is a valuable source of energy. Share *Water Power* by Ian Graham. Collect a variety of books for children to become familiar with possible new sources of energy. Ask children to choose one possible new source of energy and create a poster to make others aware of it. If you can

obtain permission, display the posters in community buildings so a larger audience becomes aware of other possible energy sources.

Simple Space & Flight Experiments by Louis Loeschnig
Expectations: Design/construct an air-powered device
For the experiment "High Rollers: A Big Wind!" you need two toilet paper rolls, a flat steady table, and a straw. Place the two cardboard tubes about 2.5 cm away from each other. With the straw, blow a steady stream of air between them. (Place the tubes on a thick, heavy book to raise the experiment higher off the table, and make it easier to do.) The stream of air blown through the straw causes the two cardboard rolls to come together.

Experiment With Air by Bryan Murphy
Expectations: Forms of energy
Moving air as a source of energy
Ask students to think about what things can be carried by air. Discuss why children think air could move these things. Ask students to think about the different ways many objects move through the air and sort and classify them into groups. Students may use well-defined categories such as objects that are thrown through the air with force (balls) or things that propel themselves through the air, such as airplanes. Students may also choose to make up their own categories instead. Share in the large group and discuss moving air as a source of energy.

Experiment With Water by Bryan Murphy
Expectations: Forms of energy
Moving water as a source of energy
Have available five copies of *Experiment With Water*. Ask students to work in pairs and select one experiment they would like to share with their Science Buddy. Have each pair collect up the materials and equipment they need to do the experiment. Children discuss how to do the experiment with their Science Buddy. At the end, they consider the results of the experiment. The children ask the Science Buddy to explain what they learned from the experiment, and write a summary with them.

Experiments With Water by Ray Brockel
Expectations: Forms of energy
Moving water as a source of energy
Fill a household-sized pail with water and place it on a table, counter, or chair. Place a second empty pail of the floor nearby. Insert one end of a meter long clear plastic hose (no kinks or crimps) into the water so it is near the bottom of the pail. Suck on the end of the hose to get the water flowing and direct it into the empty pail. Alter the height of the exit end of the hose above the second pail and notice how much water comes out at different levels. Why does more water come out when the end of the hose is closer to the pail on the floor? How does this compare with the water supply in our cities and towns? How can this same principle be used to make hydro-electricity?

If We Could See The Air by David Suzuki. Stoddart Kids

Experiments With Water by Ray Brockel. Children's Press

Windy Day Stories and Poems by Caroline Bauer. Lippincott

Let's Look At Things That Go by Nicola Tuxworth. Lorenz

Water Projects by John Williams. Raintree

The Usborne Illustrated Encyclopedia Science & Technology by Max Parsonage and Tom Petersen. Usborne

Fun With Science Air by Brenda Walpole. Warwick Press

Usborne First Science — Science Surprises by Gaby Waters. Highgate

Science In Action — Air, Air Everywhere by Tom Johnston. Gareth Stevens

Air In Action by Robin Kerrod. Cherrytree Books

The Visual Dictionary of Physics by Jack Challoner. Stoddart

Author/Title/Type	Basic Concepts	Science Process Skills	Equipment Used
Experiments With Water *Brockel, Ray* *(Discovery & Exploration)*	Energy Technology	Communicating Measuring Manipulating equipment & materials Making models	Wide variety of tools & equipment for making kites
Kites — Magic Wishes That Fly Up To The Sky *Demi, T.* *(Discovery & Exploration)*	Energy Technology	Communicating Measuring Manipulating equipment & materials Making models	Wide variety of tools & equipment for making kites
Science With Air *Edom, Helen* *(Discovery & Exploration)*	Energy Technology	Observing Communicating Experimenting Manipulating equipment & materials Making models	Measuring tools Wide variety of hands-on equipment & materials
Science With Water *Edom, Helen & Moira Butterfield* *(Discovery & Exploration)*	Energy Technology Time	Observing Communicating Experimenting Manipulating equipment & materials Making models	Measuring tools Wide variety of hands-on equipment & materials
I Wonder Why the Wind Blows & Other Questions About Our Planet *Ganeri, Anita* *(Inquiry)*	Energy Interrelationships	Interpreting Communicating	
Water Power *Graham, Ian* *(Information)*	Energy Conservation	Communicating	
Simple Space & Flight Experiments *Loeschnig, Louis* *(Discovery & Exploration)*	Energy Technology	Experimenting Interpreting Manipulating equipment & materials Making models	Large variety of materials & equipment
Experiment With Air *Murphy, Bryan* *(Discovery & Exploration)*	Energy Technology	Experimenting Interpreting Manipulating equipment & materials Making models	Balance scale Other measuring tools Wide variety of hands- on equipment & materials
Experiment With Water *Murphy, Bryan* *(Discovery & Exploration)*	Energy Technology	Experimenting Interpreting Manipulating equipment & materials Making models	Balance scale Other measuring tools Wide variety of hands- on equipment & materials
The Jumbo Book of Science *The Ontario Science Centre* *(Discovery & Exploration)*	Energy Technology	Experimenting Interpreting Manipulating equipment & materials	Large variety of materials & equipment

| _____ **Strand** | | | **TEMPLATE for** |
| Topic:_____ | | | **ORGANIZING BOOKS** |

Author/Title/Type	**Basic Concepts**	**Science Process Skills**	**Equipment Used**

6

Five Strands Together — Cross Connections

Essential science learning for children has always included skills, content, knowledge, and habits of mind or attitudes. Students who went on to higher-level science courses developed an awareness of the connections between topics and science disciplines. In today's climate, exploring these connections from the very first science lesson is an integral component of children's science learning. This chapter of *Literature and Science Breakthroughs* examines the literature-based approach to science and how it lends itself to planning, teaching, and learning through integrating topics from the five science strands.

Living Things Literature

In my previous book Imagine — a literature-based approach to science, *I developed a theme about "Living Things." The topics that evolved from this central theme included Plants, Insects, Birds, Animals, and Humans. I selected books that supported the umbrella theme, but which also gave children hands-on experiences and in-depth information about the topics.*

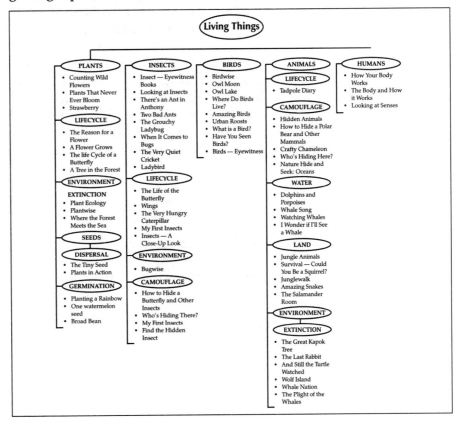

"Five strands at once? It sounds like a lot of work!" The good news: It doesn't have to be!

An integrated approach offers both you and your children a variety of benefits.

The Advantages of Integrating the Strands

1. *Integration ensures learning is unified.*

Pre-planning for the development of specific skills, content, knowledge, and attitudes through a common theme in a cross-curricular manner helps to make meaningful by identifying holistic connections to subject areas and themes.

Books from the Structures and Materials strand, for example, *Finding Out About How Things Are Built* by Helen Edom and *Up Goes The Skyscraper!* by Gail Gibbons work to strengthen a math connection. Edom's book explains how houses, skyscrapers, and bridges are constructed as she weaves the topic of measurement throughout the text and illustrations. Using this book can provide opportunities for children to extend their mathematical experiences. *This Is My House* by Arthur Dorros initiates a social studies connection when children are invited to learn more about different kinds of houses around the world. Other books based on the theme of human-made structures will add to the children's understanding and unify their learning.

2. *Integration provides an environment where science concepts are more easily understood.*

Brainstorming concepts for a specific theme and searching for the literature to support those concepts is a challenging task. The Life Science strand in *Literature and Science Breakthroughs* explores the concept of adaptation through a series of recommended books on animals. *The Night Book* by Pamela Hickman explores nature after dark with activities, experiments and information. *The Science of Living Things — How do Animals Adapt?* by Bobbie Kalman and *Where Are The Night Animals?* by Mary Ann Fraser can be used together to clarify children's understanding of "adaptation." They offer an easy-to-understand explanation and a context for exploring the concept. Children learn and confirm science concepts through a variety of integrated activities that are natural extensions of the literature. When learning has a context, it is even more meaningful.

3. *Integration offers a wide range of opportunity for language development within a meaningful context.*

The literature-based approach to teaching science encourages children to read for meaning and to select suitable resources to meet their individual language needs. Books such as *First Field Guide — Rocks and Minerals* by Edward Ricciuti and Margaret Carruthers, *Eyewitness Books — Rocks and Minerals* by Dr. R. F. Symes, *Collecting Things* by Kate Needham, *The Magic School Bus Inside the Earth* by Joanna Cole and *Milo and the Magical Stones* all enhance language development through a variety of literary styles. Simultaneously, they all focus on the study of rocks and minerals.

4. *Integration encourages a balance between teacher-directed and child-initiated learning experiences.*

Planning for integration involves a partnership between the teacher and the students. The teacher uses guidelines to identify what the children need to know. But students are involved in the process when the teacher asks them, "What do you already know about the theme? What would you like to know?" Sometimes involving a third party, such as a parent/guardian, is appropriate. This two-way (sometimes three-way) interaction during the development stages of planning a unit of study helps children hone their decision-making and problem-solving skills, which are at the heart of all learning.

5. *Integration ensures that children will be doing science in your classroom.*

When you integrate topics, you can identify and discuss hands-on instruments that are used in several science disciplines. Stars belong to the Earth and Space strand, but also to a study of instruments that help us see. Similarly, concepts may also overlap. Learning to explore the properties of matter and materials has great significance to how they can be used in structures.

Familiarity with the literature and the hands-on experiences within and among the science strands are the key to unlocking the many ways science can be explored and experienced in the classroom. When you know what books are available and what opportunities for activities they offer, you can select the ones that provide children with the best opportunities to do hands-on science investigations. The literature-based charts and the organizer within each strand present key information such as skills, concepts, expectations, and book type that will help you in the planning process. A reproducible template for the organizer is included for developing other topics.

6. *Integration invites in-depth planning and enables teachers and students to organize for success in science teaching and learning.*

Developing interdisciplinary units commands a high degree of organization. The Living Things Flow Chart on page 109 is an example of the connections that can be made between resources in the planning and development of any interdisciplinary unit.

Teachers using the science/literature approach become more confident in teaching science. "We have really changed our thinking about science. We have been doing science all along, but we just didn't realize it."

The science/literature connection gives children the opportunity to experience science in many ways. When you plan, new books can motivate you to think in new ways, to come up with new ideas. *Literature and Science Breakthroughs* provides a new way to think about and teach science. A literature-based approach has the potential to highlight connections across all five science strands. It will also help students to organize, connect, and apply their science learning in meaningful ways in their own lives.

This approach begins with planning around a theme or concept. Identify a broad-based concept such as time, change, growth, or technology, then select a topic or idea inherent in the concept. Involve your students in the planning and brainstorm a wide variety of topics with them, based on the theme you select. Encourage the children to make interdisciplinary connections during the brainstorming session. Use these connections to integrate topics as you teach. Provide books and activities that relate to both the broad-based concept and to the satellite topics from other strands.

As you research the literature, look for new books — and old favorites. Explore ideas as you search for books. Invite the children to bring you books they find about the topic. Use sharing time and magazine or newspaper articles to help the children link the world of science with the real world outside the school, and back again to the books and activities your children do.

An Example of Five Strands at Work at Once

I have selected "movement" as my broad-based concept. In the past, I have provided children with a lot of experiences emerging from this concept. I thought it would be fun to explore "movement" once again, but, this time, for its potential to cross all five science strands, while providing worthwhile science experiences for children. There are many concepts inherent in movement, and it was difficult to arrive at just one topic or idea. Perhaps it was my recent trip to the fair that suddenly made me think of spinning — and its many "interpretations": circular motion, gyration, revolution, twirl, spin. What one word or idea should I use? I selected the word "spinners" because I could develop several connections across all five science strands.

I began with the Life Systems strand, noting the topic animal growth and change. I thought about the learning expectations for this topic: characteristics of animal groups, group/classify animals, investigate how animals change, investigate how animals adapt to their environment, and observe life process of an animal. Immediately, spiders and how they spin their beautiful webs came to mind. Here was the connection I could explore. "Spiders" have a strong association with "spinners." Dangling from delicate webs, spiders could be placed under the umbrella concept: movement.

In the Matter and Materials strand, I reflected on properties of objects and materials. The learning expectations include materials commonly used, use of materials in technology, properties of substances, possible uses of these materials. Once again, I thought about spiders and the silk threads they use to make their webs. This led me to explore properties of fabrics. It seemed fitting to include the properties of fabrics, such as wool, silk, cotton, and linen as a connecting thought. Children could study various fabrics, looking at the composition and thickness of thread and, perhaps, a look at water resistant materials.

A Literature-based Web
Five Strands at Once — SPINNERS

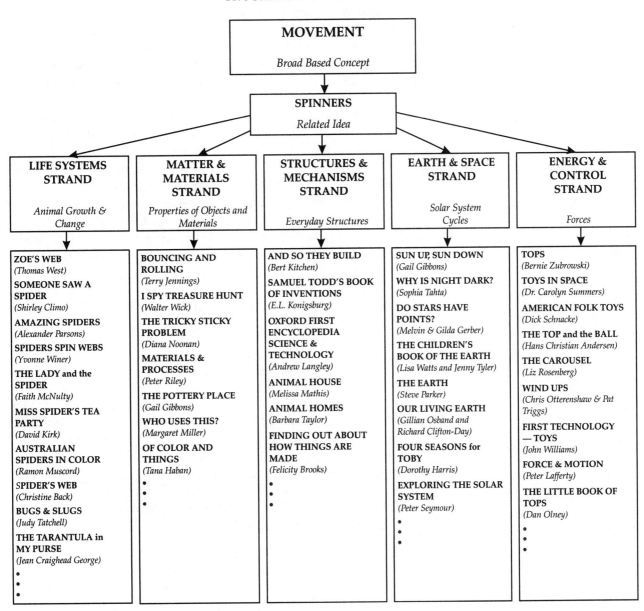

MOVEMENT

Broad Based Concept

SPINNERS

Related Idea

LIFE SYSTEMS STRAND	**MATTER & MATERIALS STRAND**	**STRUCTURES & MECHANISMS STRAND**	**EARTH & SPACE STRAND**	**ENERGY & CONTROL STRAND**
Animal Growth & Change	*Properties of Objects and Materials*	*Everyday Structures*	*Solar System Cycles*	*Forces*

ZOE'S WEB *(Thomas West)*	**BOUNCING AND ROLLING** *(Terry Jennings)*	**AND SO THEY BUILD** *(Bert Kitchen)*	**SUN UP, SUN DOWN** *(Gail Gibbons)*	**TOPS** *(Bernie Zubrowski)*
SOMEONE SAW A SPIDER *(Shirley Climo)*	**I SPY TREASURE HUNT** *(Walter Wick)*	**SAMUEL TODD'S BOOK OF INVENTIONS** *(E.L. Konigsburg)*	**WHY IS NIGHT DARK?** *(Sophia Tahta)*	**TOYS IN SPACE** *(Dr. Carolyn Summers)*
AMAZING SPIDERS *(Alexander Parsons)*	**THE TRICKY STICKY PROBLEM** *(Diana Noonan)*	**OXFORD FIRST ENCYCLOPEDIA SCIENCE & TECHNOLOGY** *(Andrew Langley)*	**DO STARS HAVE POINTS?** *(Melvin & Gilda Gerber)*	**AMERICAN FOLK TOYS** *(Dick Schnacke)*
SPIDERS SPIN WEBS *(Yvonne Winer)*	**MATERIALS & PROCESSES** *(Peter Riley)*	**ANIMAL HOUSE** *(Melissa Mathis)*	**THE CHILDREN'S BOOK OF THE EARTH** *(Lisa Watts and Jenny Tyler)*	**THE TOP and the BALL** *(Hans Christian Andersen)*
THE LADY and the SPIDER *(Faith McNulty)*	**THE POTTERY PLACE** *(Gail Gibbons)*	**ANIMAL HOMES** *(Barbara Taylor)*	**THE EARTH** *(Steve Parker)*	**THE CAROUSEL** *(Liz Rosenberg)*
MISS SPIDER'S TEA PARTY *(David Kirk)*	**WHO USES THIS?** *(Margaret Miller)*	**FINDING OUT ABOUT HOW THINGS ARE MADE** *(Felicity Brooks)*	**OUR LIVING EARTH** *(Gillian Osband and Richard Clifton-Day)*	**WIND UPS** *(Chris Otterenshaw & Pat Triggs)*
AUSTRALIAN SPIDERS IN COLOR *(Ramon Muscord)*	**OF COLOR AND THINGS** *(Tana Haban)*	• • •	**FOUR SEASONS for TOBY** *(Dorothy Harris)*	**FIRST TECHNOLOGY — TOYS** *(John Williams)*
SPIDER'S WEB *(Christine Back)*	• • •		**EXPLORING THE SOLAR SYSTEM** *(Peter Seymour)*	**FORCE & MOTION** *(Peter Lafferty)*
BUGS & SLUGS *(Judy Tatchell)*			• • •	**THE LITTLE BOOK OF TOPS** *(Dan Olney)*
THE TARANTULA in MY PURSE *(Jean Craighead George)*				• • •
• •				

In the Structure and Mechanisms strand, a study of everyday structures emphasizes the following learning expectations: shapes in structures, design/construct structures, explain functions, use of fasteners, and action/response in simple systems. Here the study of different kinds of spider webs (shapes, sizes, textures) would make an interesting focus that integrated the core idea. (Shapes — circles, ovals, squares, and triangles — could also be extended to math.)

One of the topics the Earth and Space strand focuses on is the solar system. The associated learning expectations include: models of the solar system and characteristics of planets, characteristics of the four seasons , daily/seasonal cycles, and sunlight and shadows. Each of these expectations are related to the topic "cycles." The Earth is one of nine planets that orbit the Sun. As the Earth circles the Sun, it "spins like a top that is tilted over"; it turns on its axis and tilts towards or away from the Sun.

Learning expectations from the Energy and Control strand include: how forces act on objects, observing of different forms of energy, and designing/constructing devices that use energy. Here, children could study an actual spinning top. Tops intrigue people, young and old, and can be linked to the forces that make them move, and their source of energy. And they can be linked bact to the other strands: the structure of tops, the spinning Earth and seasons, cycles, spider webs, how a spider makes its web and what the web is made of. And finally, full circle, to the spiders themselves: What kind of animal is it? How does it live? How am *I* connected to it?

The literature-based web, Five Strands At Once — Spinners, provides a good start for gathering the literature to develop the topic and tailor it according to your needs.

I continue to be passionate about finding new literature and hands-on instruments to motivate teachers to teach science and children to learn science. That was the motivation for this book. I have observed "the love of science" through the eyes of my grandchildren Benjamin, Noah, and Avery, and the many children I have taught. The art of literature draws children into discoveries about their world, instilling in them a sense of wonder and freedom of imagination. The "love of science" inspires children to run out into the school yard and in Suzuki style, "Gather monarch butterflies on milkweed plants and bring them into the school and watch them pupate and emerge from the pupa."

INDEX